W9-CKA-311

Kellie JOYce Edition

The Wait

National Library of Canada Cataloguing in Publication Data

ISBN: 978-0-9938501-0-3

JOYce, Kellie

The Wait: a memoir/ Kellie JOYce

First edition, 2014

Ordering Information: www.kelliejoyce.ca
BLOG: kelliejoyce.blogspot.ca

Kellie JOYce

Some of the proceeds from this book will be donated to DUNARA in Guelph, Ontario.

What people are saying about *The Wait*

Spellbound and riveting, Kellie bravely bares her soul. The impact of this book will be felt for years to come by people from all walks of life. PTSD (Post Traumatic Stress Disorder) can be set in motion silently, the causes are numerous. This book may be the wake-up call to the medical community to better understand mental illness and its many facets.
Serge Poirier, Retired Military

I had the honour of being the first editor to read the opening pages of Kellie's book. I was just a few pages in when I knew, without a doubt, that this story needed to be told. Kellie has had harrowing, difficult times and has the emotional scars to prove it. Yet, in spite of it all, she continues to live life with a vivacious spirit that should be an inspiration to anyone mired in the quicksands of emotional crisis. It's a powerful story, powerfully told in a voice that rings convincing and true.
Geoff Meeker, Writer and Editor

The Wait is a story of an individual destined to make her mark on the world. Mom shares stories of struggles that are often blocked off and mostly hidden by society. In a raw and engulfing tale she brings these struggles to light.
High School Student, loving daughter, Sarah

Overcoming childhood trauma is a gift one gives to self, but it takes courage and there are many roadblocks. Most of the time the ones closest to you, such as family, understand the least. Their own denial puts up that barrier. Counselors of abuse survivors must recognize the level of support that survivors require. Their courage sometimes is not enough. It is an honour to know you Kellie and to be witness to your hard earned healing. You go girl!!!
Linda Soper, MSW RSW

Kellie JOYce has provided an honest, in depth, account of the emotional, physical and sexual abuse she suffered as a child, it's impact and her struggle for recovery. Kellie's story is one of adversity and courage. I recommend her book to anyone who wants to understand the genesis of mental illness and a brave person's fight to overcome it.
Vikas Khaladkar, Crown Attorney

Kellie Joyce's passion and dedication to work toward ending stigma and discrimination is an inspiration.
Nicholas Watters, Mental Health Knowledge Exchange Expert

Acknowledgements

During the writing of this book I received a lot of love and support from my family and friends. The numbers are too great to list all of you, but you know who you are. Thank you for listening to me, for reading my book, for your valuable feedback, and again for all your love and support.

I would, however, like to personally acknowledge the following people who helped to bring my memoir to fruition.

To my editor, Kerry Russelo. I am grateful for bumping into you that day at our local library. When I mentioned I needed an editor for the book I was writing, you spoke up and said, "I would love to edit your book." I thought I had hit the jackpot and I was right! That was the beginning of a lifelong friendship. Thanks for your great contribution. You really did help to bring my story to life.

To Luben Boykov for allowing me to use the photograph I took of his exquisite piece of art as my book's cover. I appreciate your kindness. "Luben Boykov, sculptor, Bishop Spencer School Memorial, St. John's Newfoundland, bronze, stone, 2001"

To my three good friends who helped me with computer expertise, book formatting, and cover. I thank you for your support. Leslie Plhak, Ted Poweski and Gabriel Nemeth, you are what I call 'life savers'.

To Dale Curd, host of Life Story Project on the Oprah Winfrey Network, where my story was first shared. My appearance on the show allowed my story to be available to the world. Thank you for writing my foreword. Your heartfelt thoughts were greatly appreciated and worth "the wait".

To my special friend, Serge Poirier, who, during my darkest moments when I doubted myself and my ability, believed in me and encouraged me to continue the writing of my story. I am forever indebted to you.

To my husband and three daughters who have been there through all the pain and tears. I hope this makes you proud. Thanks for your love.

I dedicate this book to the memory of a great Canadian artist and loving father. Your love and strength have guided me through the writing of this book. I have included your unedited letters in my book. Gone but not forgotten.

To my three daughters who have taught me the meaning of unconditional love.

I love you.

As I scribe my sentiments using pen and paper, I acknowledge the wisdom, strength and freedom to do so.

It is the difference between existing and living. I choose living.

Kellie JOYce

Foreword

"What I remember most about our first meeting was how separate and yet a part of her surroundings she was. Isolated, distant and yet blending in-no different from any other individual I saw, met or spoke to that day. Kellie JOYce waited, mostly in silence, for her moment to sit with me on a purple couch in the middle of busy downtown Toronto square to open up and share her story for Life Story Project.

And then Kellie spoke.

My mind reeled with the images she gave me and my heart tightened and ached and I felt that familiar pressure behind my eyes and tremor in my lower lip which meant sadness; only now I could also feel the pressure in my chest building which for me is despair.

Deep despair. The kind that makes your body heave, your throat burn and lungs fight for big gulps of air. I heard Kellie's story and I heard her tell me her life in a way that sounded like a small child standing on a stage frail, yet un-wavering and confident in the power of the truth to cut through detachment and isolation.

Why is this so in our world? Why do we make the people who tell the truth feel so alone and lonely, while we shower our attention on others who fill our life with lies? Why do we make those who know the truth work so hard to be heard?

I could tell by listening to Kellie more with my eyes than with my ears that she wasn't interested in whether I thought she was telling the truth-she knew the truth and had weathered many conversations with doubters-she had had to fight to be heard.

This is often true for those who suffer with mental illness such as depression and PTSD, they fight for us to hear them. It is we who make it hard for them to explain their reality and how it differs from ours. We are the ones who struggle to hear their pain often because their pain is so close so resonant with our own.

Reading this book will be a challenge for many and some I know will put it down thinking that it is too much too soon. I ask you who are struggling to reflect on the strength and courage of a young girl to endure, cope, confront and eventually process and heal tremendous pain. This is no extraordinary child-this is not an especially gifted or privileged individual rather, Kellie JOYce is a human being like you-a human being with a remarkable life story that has the power to reach inside you and touch what is precious inside everyone; our hope."

Dale Curd,
Host, Life Story Project
OWN Canada.

Chapter One

Today was the day I learned I had a heart that could be broken and a soul that could be destroyed. It was my ninth birthday. I had been waiting for this day for a whole year. That's a long time for a nine year old! A birthday was one of the only days when Mom did special things for us. We all looked forward to our turn as Mom would bake us a cake and the birthday kid got to lick the bowl clean. Oh, how I loved that! As an added treat Mom would bring us tea in bed. Usually one of us was told to bring tea to Mom so she could have it in bed with her morning cigarette.

I got tired of waiting in my room for Mom so I got up. I looked around. There was no sign of any birthday preparations. I wondered if Mom was planning something extra special. I was feeling so excited, but the hours passed and nothing was happening. Still, I kept wishing and hoping.

A special occasion was usually a day of rest in our house, but not today. It ended up being like any other day, just more drinking and arguing. It didn't matter that it was my birthday. *He* was the same and so was Mom. She said nothing, as always, and took whatever abuse he gave her like the good wife she was taught to be. That's what was drilled into my head every day at home and at church. I wanted to yell out, "This is BULLSHIT! Stop hurting my mom!" But I too had been taught that I should be seen, not heard.

The day was nearly over and no one had said or done anything. I was nine years old today and it didn't seem to matter to anyone. "How could my mom forget my birthday?" I asked myself. I cried silently as I felt my heart break. I felt like part of me was dying, as if I didn't exist. I just wanted the day to end.

When it came time to go to church with my neighbour, Liz, I went gladly. I kept singing, "Happy Birthday to meeee, Happy Birthday to meeee," over and over in my head. I wanted to feel happy. For a short time I did.

Chapter Two

At exactly five o'clock sharp every evening, rain or shine, Liz and I would leave for church. Liz would grab my arm and allow her frail body to be guided by me. At first Liz used to scare me to death. She was a cross old lady to everyone but me, always yelling at kids to stay off her property, to keep their sticky hands to themselves.

In our small community of Seal Rocks, Newfoundland, everyone knew everyone. Liz lived across the street from where I lived so I got to see a different side of her. She was quiet and never spoke a word to me. I liked that! As time passed I began to feel less anxious and more relaxed around her and I looked forward to our times together.

Today, like most days, our walk to church was calm and peaceful. The service allowed me to learn what 'still' meant. For that hour I was allowed to say nothing. If a child spoke in church that child would be singled out and yelled at to stop talking immediately. I surprised even myself by my silence, for I usually had so much to say.

I didn't like any of what I heard at that church. It felt like a pack of lies: cruelty, albeit in words only. But at least here nobody was acting it out like at home. I learned to appreciate and value the beauty of the peace and quiet and to feel a safety I never felt at home. So it was here, in church, that the idea to talk about my feelings in my head developed.

I am being tormented by what goes on at home. No, I don't mean siblings who bully or parents who nag me to do chores or homework. I mean things that no child

should ever witness or experience. I have quickly learned that anywhere I go, I can allow myself to plan my thoughts and write, visualizing what it is I want to say.
Not in pictures.
Just words.
Just words in my head.

I have a vision of being a writer one day. I keep saying that to myself. Of course I couldn't write my words down on paper. He wouldn't allow it. I would be beaten to a pulp if he saw my thoughts and it would make Mom's life more horrific than it already was. NO! My quiet time here in church is mine, and, as I write in my head, my story continues...

Cantankerous

It never let up
The arguments
Volatile behaviours
Commanded vigilance on my part

No time for play
No time for dreams
No time for happiness
Just time wasted

Stripped of
My innocence
My self-worth
My childhood

Imaginary Kellie
That's how I existed.

Kellie JOYce – December 2012

Chapter Three

It snowed a lot last night and when we woke up this morning the snow was piled up to the windows. Usually my older brother, Claude, would climb out the window and shovel the wet snow to make a path for us so we could walk to school. When Mom announced we would not be going to school that day, my heart sank.

"I can't send you off to school when there is nothing in your little tummies," she said.

Yesterday all we had to eat was flour mixed with water that Mom had fried on the stove. Today we didn't even have that. Winter makes it difficult for us to go out and pick the wild berries that grow in the fields and marshes that surround us. In the summertime berries were a quick fix to fill our empty stomachs, but wintertime held the cold reality that our food supply was limited.

Neither one of my parents worked, except on the rare occasions when my father went away on the boats. Like many Newfoundland families the government provided us with minimal assistance so that we could survive. How strange it was, I thought, that my parents still found ways to have enough money to buy cigarettes and booze and yet there was never enough money to buy food for us to eat.

I cried and cried because I wanted to go to school. However, my crying only ended up adding to the weakness I felt that day. And no school meant a whole extra day being around him.

"Where is God when you need Him?" I asked myself. He never answers me, kinda like Mom. It seems useless, but I still try to have a conversation with Him anyway. But, like Mom, I feel He never listens to me either.

Later that day when my brother was finished shoveling, he found two frozen rabbits buried under the snow on the front step. Mom's eyes lit up as he came running into the house and yelled, "Look what I found! Look what I found!" He was holding up the two dead rabbits by the hind legs so we all could see what he had found.

I was the only one in the family who ever asked questions. My other siblings remained silent, but I didn't. I wanted to know everything. So I asked my mom, "Where did we get the rabbits? Who left them here for us? How did they know we needed food? And why can't I go to school, Mom? I won't tell anyone I'm hungry." There was no shortage of questions and I quickly blurted them out.

"I'm not worried that you'll tell someone," my Mom snapped. "I am more worried that you will pass out at school." As usual, Mom didn't answer the rest of my questions.

That day we had rabbit stew. Not much of a stew really. The two rabbits were skinned and put in a pot filled with water, a small potato that we borrowed from Liz and a piece of onion. It tasted awful I thought, but I had no choice but to eat it. That, or go hungry. The smell of rabbit wafted throughout the house, and for days after the smell lingered.

I was still able to go to church with Liz that evening. I really thought this was strange as I wasn't allowed to go to school, but I said nothing. I did have the good sense to know when it was or wasn't a good time to ask questions, and this was one of those times. I was grateful just to be getting a chance to leave the house and feel a sense of calm. I felt badly for my siblings who had no outlet, no way to release their feelings. But I went anyway.

Liz was crying in church again today. She didn't say anything, but I could see her crying. It seemed like this happened a lot and I didn't understand. Really, why cry here? Me, I like to watch the people. And as I watched Liz, I began to feel her sadness. I wanted to ask her if she was okay, if she needed a hug, but I knew it was best not to say a word. For some reason older people don't want kids to see their pain. I don't understand that either. So I pretended not to know she was upset. But it did affect me, and as a tear rolled down my cheek, I quickly wiped it away. I had a bond with this crabby old lady, one I couldn't put into words yet. I just felt it.

This evening it took us much longer to walk home from church. On the way back Liz asked if I would mind stopping at the cemetery to visit her mom's grave. We stayed there for quite some time. I couldn't help feeling that there was something wrong, something really, really wrong!

8

Chapter Four

In the weeks following that evening Liz and I did not go to church at all. Words continued to float around in my head. They flooded my thoughts, verging on madness. I was scared of both the known and the unknown. Also I realized I missed my peaceful times with Liz.

I noticed all the other kids playing outside, riding their sleds and making snowball forts. Not my siblings and I; we weren't often allowed outside. Because Mom dotes on Dad, always making sure that his needs are met, I don't believe she notices our needs. I don't feel she is even aware that we are missing all the fun things that kids do. I wonder if she herself ever did those things as a child. She never spoke of her childhood. All I knew was that it seemed like we were the puppets and Dad pulled **all** the strings, especially Mom's.

Chapter Five

We don't visit people. If it weren't for my aunts and uncles, Mom's sisters and brothers, we would have no visitors, nor would we have ever left our house. My grandmother had seventeen children. She and my mom were having children at the same time. So it felt like I belonged to a really big family with lots of brothers and sisters. Not really uncommon in Newfoundland. Seems like that's all the women did to stay warm in the harsh winter months.

At first I was so excited when Aunt Betty and Aunt Stasha called on us today. They came to take us out to enjoy the snow. But, as always, even when we played, my mind was not at rest. I was constantly writing in my head. Even though I was enjoying the break of being outside, I could not erase the thoughts that plagued my mind. Where was Liz? And why had she disappeared? I asked my aunts quite a few times, and finally, in a very impatient voice, one of my aunts said, "Stop with all the questions and just try to enjoy your sledding, Kel!"

It was no use. I continued to question. "Please, Aunt Stasha. Please tell me why Liz isn't going to church. Is Mom hiding something from me? Is Liz dying? What is it? I want to know!"

"I really don't know, Kel," my aunt replied. "I would tell you if I knew." I believed her, as kids often do. But, as usual, we kids are the last to know anything. This was the case with Liz.

Later, when we got home from sledding, all my questions were answered. Liz had died. Mom was all dressed up to go to church. This was the only time I got to see Mom dressed up. I begged and pleaded with her to let me go.

"You can't go to church today, Kellie. It is not a good idea." But I insisted on going. I wanted to say my good-byes to Liz. I was relieved that Mom had finally told me the truth. Sad, but relieved.

This was the first time I had ever seen a dead body in a casket. Liz looked so unreal and oddly enough she had a smile on her face. Very few people saw her smile, but this was the last impression left to us. Some of the people in church were crying. But I didn't cry. I was hurting so much inside and yet I couldn't cry at all. I was angry. Liz's death meant I had no escape anymore. I would have no more daily outings of peace and stillness. I knew it wasn't her fault for dying but I felt betrayed by her anyway.

I stood around in a daze, listening to people whispering that Liz had died of breast cancer. Why was I the last one to find out? I was the one who spent time with her and loved her. These people didn't really care about her. They only came to the funeral out of respect, because that's what you did when someone died. Kids got no respect, not in my world. Didn't seem fair at all!

Although I was the only kid in the church that day, I felt like I fit in. I felt I belonged there. I don't relate well to most nine year olds and I thought about this as I looked around the room, denying myself the freedom to feel my emotions, or at least to show them. I didn't want to be a grownup yet, but I really had no choice. Liz's death had caused me to grow up faster than I wanted.

At a time like this I didn't think anyone would understand my great pain and loss, so I knew it was best to keep it to myself. In the past I had pretended I hated going to church so that my father would make me go. Liz was gone. Now what?

Chapter Six

The next day at school one of the girls, Monique, wanted me to play with her. When I asked her what we could play, she answered, "Make believe."

"How do you play that?" I asked.

She described it as a game where you pretend to see things and do things and talk to people who are not there. I thought this sounded like a stupid game and I wanted no part of it. Monique played with me anyway and she didn't try to change my mind. I liked her more for that. I liked her for not trying to force me to play her stupid game. That day I realized Monique liked me for who I was.

I smile now remembering how great that made me feel.

I told her I was a writer, not on paper, but that I wrote words in my head. She laughed out loud at me and then excitedly asked, "But can't you see pictures? Can't you pretend you are an angel with wings?"

I really thought she was being silly. I couldn't believe her. How does one see pictures of things in one's head that aren't there? To me, that was the dumbest thing ever and I wanted no part of it! (Though I wrote that down as a mental note in my thoughts.)

Later that day after I left school to go home, I tried to play Monique's pretend game on my own. I wanted to see if I could picture anything, but I couldn't. All I saw were my words. I couldn't understand why the kids at school liked this pretend game so much. It was a really popular game and I questioned why. In my brain there was no room for pretending. It was already full. Reality had a way of doing that. Besides, I wanted to be me and that was all there was to it!

To this day I am unable to visualize objects in my head. It took many years before I realized that I was different in this respect. It's like a handicap I suppose, and maybe that's why, as an adult, I enjoy photography so much. I can capture and keep images that I can't store in my memory.

Chapter Seven

I've been thinking about Liz a lot this week. I miss her! I miss my time with her. I am reminded of her when I play 'Spin the Bottle' with my aunts and uncles. At school this was also a popular game, but with my aunts and uncles it was played our special way. It was our little secret and I wasn't allowed to tell anyone.

We would jump over the fence to Liz's property. Now that she was dead it was easier for us to play our game. We knew she wasn't going to chase after us, as she often did, trying to hit us with her BB gun. Her property was mostly a wooded area. We would go to our favourite spot and the eight of us would sit around in a circle and put a Coke bottle in the middle. We would take turns spinning it. We had played it so often that the ground was worn where we placed the bottle. The person who spun the bottle got to take the person it pointed to behind the trees where no one else could see. That person had to do whatever was asked. If we were two girls behind the trees, we would mostly just giggle. But it was different when it was a boy and a girl. I was usually asked to take off my pants and show my private parts. Sometimes the boys would want to touch them or want me to touch theirs. I didn't think this was such a big deal. I was used to seeing my father's penis all the time. His was a lot bigger, that's for sure.

Today when we played our secret game, my Uncle Mike, the oldest at seventeen, asked me to turn around so he could see my bum. I, being only nine years old, thought this was a strange request, but I quickly showed him, pulled up my pants and ran back to the circle.

15

This wasn't the way we played the game at school. We never played it the special way. At school it was just a talking game. But on Liz's property among the trees, it was something totally different and secret.

Chapter Eight

I am good at keeping secrets. Mom stressed that it was not such a good thing to do. I thought it was because she was awful at it. She was so frank and honest with her feelings. Mom really hated lies. If we lied to her, she would be so angry. However, because I had seen what telling the truth could do, I often lied.

One day I took ninety-five cents that Mom had left on the end table in our living room. I had seen it there for a few days and I thought that Mom had forgotten about it. So I stole it to buy treats. When Mom discovered the money was missing, we three older kids were placed on our knees in the corner with our schoolbooks on our heads. We were made to stay there for hours. I finally confessed because my knees were raw from the cracks in the wooden floor. Were my two brothers mad at me! Not only had I caused them to be punished, I had not even shared my treats with them. My father gloated when giving me the belt. The welts left across my bum made it hard for me to sit at school. But I said nothing of what had happened, remembering instead how good it felt to pig out on that junk food.

It is still a sweet memory and causes me to chuckle out loud.

After that I was blamed for everything. It didn't matter whether or not I was telling the truth. So lies became easy for me. At times, necessary!

17

Chapter Nine

It was not long after Liz's death that Mom was diagnosed with cancer. The news filled me with fear. The doctors told her that the cancer was in the very early stages and that she would be okay. Still I was frightened! Mom was told she would have to go to St. John's for surgery and would be away from us for over a week. St. John's is Newfoundland's capital city. That's where most people have to go when it is a complicated medical emergency. It was about a ten hour car ride from where we lived. Of course I was worried for my mom, but I was also afraid for my sisters and me. I was just nine years old and my sisters were five and seven. I was not as worried about my brothers because my father generally left them alone. Knowing that we would be left in his care for the whole time Mom was gone played havoc in my mind.

I could barely sleep during the weeks we waited for Mom to go for surgery. I tried to hide my fear from her. She had enough to worry about and must have felt scared herself. She didn't notice that anything was wrong and that the five of us were worried that she would not return.

I have two brothers and two sisters. Claude was the oldest by two years. Everyone called him the bastard child, born before my mom got married.

I was the next oldest, born at seven months. I spent the first six weeks of my life in an incubator, struggling to survive. I was later told that I was born early because my father, beat my mom, causing her to go into early labour. I never asked her about this. I guess I really didn't want

18

to know, as there were already so many truths I wish I'd rather not known.

Yet today this ranks highly on my list of great sadness.

My younger brother, Steven, was born eleven months later. He was the quiet one and only spoke when asked a question. He was the fairest kid I ever knew, always wanting to treat everyone the same. In fact I only ever saw Steven angry when he addressed our father's prejudiced tongue. My father, however, would quickly silence him with a quick slap across the face.

Then came Jessy. She was the odd one out. Big, beautiful blue eyes, a perfect smile, but not my father's child. This was confirmed many times during Dad's drunken evenings when he would beat my mother until she was black and blue. We all got to see and hear those fights. So it was no secret that Jessy was not our full blood sister. It was also no secret that Mom treated her differently. Mom would say that Jessy needed more attention because she was born with a hole in her heart called a heart murmur. But we all knew that was not the reason. We knew that Mom favoured Jessy because she didn't belong to our father.

Margaret was the baby. It hurts to write this, but I don't know her. The little I have seen of her as an adult reminds me of a part of myself...LOST!

Our house had four tiny rooms. There were two bedrooms, one for my parents and the other was shared by the five of us. Two single beds barely fit in our room. We three girls snuggled in one bed while my two brothers shared the other. A ten-gallon bucket in the corner of our bedroom was what we called the bathroom. It was emptied daily into an outhouse that the wind often blew over.

We had no running water. There was a small wood stove in the space we called a kitchen, but there were many cold winter days and nights when we had no wood to burn. In the winter we filled in the cracks around the windows and the door, and even the walls of the house, with whatever cloth we could find. At night my sisters and I hugged each other tightly to stay warm. Some nights the five of us would be in one bed trying to use our bodies as a blanket to keep in the heat.

Mom asked me to tell my sisters that she was going to the hospital. "You're the oldest," she said, "so you'll have to take my place while I'm away."

It was something I really didn't want to do. But I did. I tried my best to comfort them and tell them that Mom would be okay and would only be gone for a short time and then she would return. I was surprised that the news of Mom's illness didn't have the same effect on them as it did on me. Of course, they were younger and probably didn't fully understand. But I did! I remembered Liz.

Funny enough, at times I really did feel like their mom and not their sister. I fell into that role without a choice, and I wonder how I learned to do it. No one told me; no one showed me. Yet I took on the caretaker role quite naturally. I even got my sisters to play that stupid game of pretend that Monique had taught me! They quite enjoyed it and that annoyed me, although I didn't let it show. So, in a way, I guess I too was pretending.

The next day at school I told Monique about it. She thought it was funny and chuckled. "That's not exactly the same thing, Kellie," she said. But for me this was the closest to make believe I was gonna get! However, I must admit that this game really caused me some confusion because part of me really wanted to play.

Chapter Ten

"Please come out from behind the piano, Kellie." Ms. Darling spoke softly. "Come on now. Be brave. Be brave."

I had to be brave every day of my life at home. At school I just wanted to be me. At school I wasn't told to shut up. I wasn't called stupid. And I wasn't forced to do anything I didn't want to do. So, if I didn't want to have a needle, no one was gonna make me.

I was the only one in my class who was tiny enough to fit through the small space to hide behind the piano. At ten years of age I weighed about fifty-four pounds. I was the target and the laughing stock of my class. Most days this bothered me, even though I was called a lot worse at home. It hurt that my friends made fun of me, but not today. It didn't bother me at all. I was the clever one. I had found a way to escape the needle. That gave me some instant pleasure.

I sat behind the piano for what seemed like hours, listening to kids screaming and crying. Well, I guess I wasn't really listening, but I'm not sure where I went. It felt as if I were no longer in the room. I could faintly hear my classmates, but it didn't faze me. Not one bit!

I stayed behind the piano all afternoon until I heard the bell ring. I believe I even fell asleep for a short while. I heard Ms. Darling say, "It's okay to come out now, Kellie. It's safe. Everyone is gone." Finally I snapped out of my trance-like state, bolted from behind the piano, grabbed my things and headed home.

I sang and laughed out loud along the way. This was the second time that the school nurse had come to give us our booster shot and I had escaped it again. I was having a great conversation with myself. "Now who is controlling whom?" I so enjoyed my inner chats. I continued them until I got home. I felt great and I said nothing of the day's events at school.

Chapter Eleven

We weren't allowed to go to school much this week. It was the week that we received our welfare cheque and, as usual, my father disappeared with it and Mom was left to fend for us.

It was peaceful not having him at home for a few days while he was drinking away our grocery money. The anticipation of his return, however, tormented my brain.

Mom did what she had to do to survive and to keep us fed. It didn't take me long to figure out how we got our food. It became a pattern I was able to follow. I met all her lovers. They tried to be nice to us so we wouldn't tell my father that they had been at our house while he was away. It didn't matter though because he would beat the truth out of Mom when he got home. We would sit up in our beds listening, crying and secretly wanting to die. At least I did. My older brother sometimes tried to help Mom, but my father would just sling him across the room. There were bullies at school, but none as mean as my father. He was the biggest bully of all. I was embarrassed to say he was my father, ashamed that I shared the same blood.

My mom smiled today, like she did most days when he was gone. It is one of the few memories I have of her smiling. I sat there watching her with Myron, asking myself if she was really happy or if she was just pretending like Monique wanted me to do. Is she seeing pictures in her head of being married to a prince who comes and sweeps her off her feet, who brings her gifts and tells her how beautiful she is? I wasn't sure, so I asked, "Mom, are you in love with Myron?" They both laughed so hard.

"No, honey," she said. "We're just friends."

After that I got the same response every time I asked. But I never stopped asking. I was confused. I had heard talk of love at school. Kids would say they loved each other. I would see people holding hands and kissing. Was that love? The closest I saw of love in my house was my mom and her friends laughing together. I figured people in love laughed together and did nice things for each other, like when Myron brought us food. At ten years of age my mind wasn't made up yet. I couldn't really figure out what love was and what it felt like to love someone. I thought about Liz. I loved her, but it was not the same kind of love my mom had for her friends. Maybe there are different kinds of love I told myself. One day I want to know them all.

Chapter Twelve

There was a different feeling in our house the few times my father went away to work on the boats. Mom acted like a wild cat that had been locked in a cage and then set free. She became more like a show cat for all her friends. I was jealous of them because they got to share a part of my mother that I only got to observe from the sidelines. Mom wouldn't talk to me, yet she spent hours talking and laughing with these strange men who came to visit. They were strange to me, but not to my mother. It seemed like my father was away for a few months duration, and, for that period of time, we had plenty of food to eat. Of course, Mom had no shortage of cigarettes, drugs and alcohol, or men for that matter.

Claude, my older brother, was starting to become a part of that scene. As I watched him in astonishment from the corner of our little shack, a smoke in one hand, a drink in the other, I was confused. I couldn't believe my mother was there, laughing with her friends, while Claude was getting high and drunk. Once again Mom said nothing. She allowed it. I wanted my mother to care more and to see what was happening around us, but she was blind to it all. I wondered if she did as I did. If, in her head, she escaped to a place where she felt disconnected, unaware and safe. Watching Claude forced me to want to go there. I didn't mind at all. I liked the world of words that I would create in my head. So I tuned everyone out. It was as easy as flipping a switch.

"Would you like to taste it, Karkey?" he asked.

"You're nuts," I replied. "That's the last thing I want."

26

"Come on, Karkey. Have a drink," Claude kept chanting. He thought it was hilarious to call me that. It was a nickname he had created for me. When he was younger he tried saying car keys and Kellie at the same time and came up with Karkey. I was stuck with it! He kept talking to me; I kept writing.

There were several empty rum bottles around the house when I awoke. My brother had already left, in a rage and angry. Mom's friend, Ray, had stayed over and was still in her room when we got ready for school. I actually liked Ray. He was genuine. Well, I felt he was. He took a liking to me because of my sense of humour that I felt free to show when he was around. That, plus he made Mom happy. I thought this to myself, but I would never say it out loud to Mom. I wished Dad would never come home. I wished Ray could be my dad. My brother called him a fucking asshole. I knew these were bad words that I should not repeat. "He is not!" I answered. "I like him."

Mom acted as though she didn't hear us at all during that conversation. Perhaps that was a good thing.

"Just stop, Mom, STOP! We don't want to hear any more!"

I had started to read some of my story to my two teenage daughters. They think it's great that their mom wants to be a writer. Even though they feel that my writing may be fabulous, they find the content disturbing and sad. By their response I could see that this was too much for them to process. They live in a world of love, security and much opportunity.

Kellie JOYce

I guess as I write this story, as it flows from my pen to paper, I, too, am a little saddened. But if the truth were known, I'm not unhappy enough to stop. The sad little girl in me is begging to be heard. She has always wanted to write. The only way I can be stopped now is if I can no longer see the words. But they are still there, ready to be written and shared. So I forge ahead, without my daughters' input. In my story I don't see the depth of sadness and pain involved, or even the great losses. All I see are the words that, when released from my head, bring peace to my heart and soul. It makes me happy actually. Words have always made me happy. Not make believe though, just the real stuff. I want to keep it real.

Chapter Thirteen

My brother and I were returning from the water well one Saturday morning when we saw a petite, well-dressed lady with big glasses knocking on our door. We didn't have people visiting us very often so I was curious to know who she was. I dropped my bucket of water and quickly ran and hid under the front step so I could hear everything that was being said. She said that she had come for a 'home visit' and went inside the house with my mom. I heard the lady saying my name as she was explaining about the needle I needed to get. I became frustrated when Mom closed the door and I could no longer hear any more of what was being said.

After that the lady visited our house every Saturday for three weeks in a row, but she didn't talk about the needle any more. Mom sat us all down and explained that our house was deemed as being 'unfit living conditions'. None of us knew what that meant. Then she hit us with the news. We were going to move to a new house, one with running water, a bathroom, three bedrooms and a lot more space. She hesitated before telling us the bad part. We would be moving to a new town, away from all of our family and friends.

Children's Aid Services, as Mom called them, had come into our home, torn it apart and deemed the house unfit. I thought I was to blame. I was angry with myself. If I had been given that needle, we wouldn't have to move. Children's Aid would not have come to our house and would not have seen how we lived. I was making my mom cry. She cried enough from all of her beatings and the frustrations of trying to provide for us. And now, after giving us the news, she cried even more. She didn't want to move away. She said her sisters and brothers needed her; her family and friends needed her. I believe she needed them more.

I didn't believe in God any more since He had taken Liz from me, but I prayed that He would take me away as well. I wanted Mom's pain to stop.

Waiting

Here I am, God
Reading this banner
Hanging on the side of me
It says,' Thank you God for Life'
As I can plainly see.
Well, I want to thank You, God,
For this life I'm supposed to lead.
But I'm afraid to ask, "What life?"
You know my feelings indeed
I'm living in terror and pain, God.
Why can't You understand?
Please take me up in heaven with You.
Give me a helping hand.
I don't see any reason to live this way.
Please look at my point of view.
Please take me and guard the way
Because, God, I am depending on You.
Please don't fail, God, on this little task
Take me up in heaven with You
That's all I'll ever ask.
Show me the way, God, and open the door
I don't want to wait any more.

Kellie JOYce – January 1979

Chapter Fourteen

I am relieved that we have school today. Sometimes the words crowd my head and I just have to get them down. I never use any of the bad words my family uses. The fear of a ruler being whipped across my bum is a good motivator.

I like my Grade 6 teacher, Ms. Lowery. She allows me to write during class. Sometimes she reads my poetry to the kids. Afterwards they usually applaud very loudly, and inside I feel worthy, as if I have a purpose. It makes me feel human, even if only for a short while.

I became known at school for my poetry writing. I was also known for my speeches. I had found a way to express myself and I really liked it. A couple of times I even won some small cash prizes.

I was most happy when I got to write in class. I believe Ms. Lowery saw that. Sometimes I would be surprised, like when she announced to the class that I had won another poetry contest. I never knew anything about it until it was shared with all of us. At the beginning of the school year Ms. Lowery had asked me if she could enter some of my poems in the contests that might come up across the island. I saw no reason to say no. If she was about to help me, I would be willing to do the same. So I kept writing poems for Ms. Lowery for many years following, even when she was no longer my teacher.

I don't believe the kids ever found my poetry depressing, not like my own daughters do. But then again, I was very selective in what I expressed.

Chapter Fifteen

Today my father returned from the boats. He claimed he had missed his family. It was exciting for maybe an hour because he returned with lots of food and treats for Mom and for us. It seemed that he brought home enough cigarettes and alcohol to last a year. However, it would be lucky if these lasted a week in our house. Mom and Dad drank the booze like coffee all day long while they smoked the cigarettes.

Dad brought this big man home from the boats. He gave each of us a dollar. At first I thought he was nice. Later, when they were all drunk, he ended up having sex with my mom. When he passed out, it was my father's turn and he beat her while doing so. I tried singing with my sisters as all this was going on. I wished I could take them to this place in my mind where I go when I write.

This is how a lot of those days went: drinking, drugs, sex, different men with my mom and then the beatings. You kinda get used to it, you know. It didn't seem right to me, but I knew not to question it. Kids weren't supposed to question their parents, but I did. When I asked Mom, she made excuses for him and said, "Your father just gets angry when he drinks, honey. Mom is okay."

That's all I saw, all I knew, and it was the only reassurance I ever got from my mother. I used to talk to my aunts and uncles about what was happening at home, but it seemed they knew. "Just don't think about all that stuff, my love," my Aunt Stasha would say. I thought that was a strange thing to tell a ten year old. How could I not think about it when it was my whole existence?

Chapter Sixteen

My mom's father and siblings lived only minutes from our house. To get there you went straight out the door to the left and up a long lane. The week after we were told we were moving, my mom went to tell her family. I was worried about Mom and followed her up the lane to Grandfather's. He was outside and waved Mom over to see him in the wood shed. He closed the door. I listened with my ear pressed tightly to the window and I heard my mom apologizing to her father. I couldn't really understand why she was doing that. It became evident quite quickly.

In those moments that followed, as I sat curled up in a ball outside the shed, I could hear my mother and her father having sex. I knew what I was hearing. I had heard my mother having sex with other men many times before. But with her father? I felt disgusted and something inside me told me this was wrong. She didn't cry for him to stop as she often did when my father had sex with her. She didn't say he was hurting her either. By the sounds she was making it seemed as if it brought her great pleasure.

I quietly got up and ran into the house where my Aunt Susan was taking bread out of the oven. She offered me a fresh hot slice with butter and molasses and I quickly gobbled it down.

Aunt Susan was now the one in the house taking on the role of being a mother. You see, my grandmother had died of a stroke, caused by high blood pressure, when the youngest of the seventeen children, Idamae, was only two. My mom often said that she herself had previously taken on this role because she was the oldest of her siblings. That day I had a clearer understanding of what she meant by that.

I tried in my head to make sense of what I had learned. For the first time in my life I couldn't even see words. My body felt so sick and shaky and later that evening I actually threw up. I blamed it on the hot bread that I had devoured at my grandfather's place, but I knew darn well that it was because of what I had heard.

I did not sleep well that night. My mind was trying to understand. I went to school the next day very tired but I acted as if nothing had happened. When the teacher asked if I would like to write I politely replied, "No, thank you." I knew I could not write about those events. I actually had no words that I could put on paper. For the first time I had drawn a blank. It remained that way for a very long time.

Chapter Seventeen

Do you ever stop to take in the beauty around you? Watch the trees change with each season? I often found myself doing this. From as early on as I can remember, I found refuge in the bounty of Newfoundland. I felt much like the trees. As I sat under one today, it gave me both shelter and comfort. Like a tree hug I suppose.

It was the 23rd day in the month of March, exactly a month until my birthday. Moving day!! Seal Rocks would no longer be my home. I was told that Corner Brook was a much bigger place, with a hospital, a mall and even a theatre. There was nothing like that in Seal Rocks. We had lived a pretty isolated and simple life. I knew my world was changing in more ways than one. I had mixed feelings but kept them to myself.

The seven of us didn't have much to pack, just a small sofa, our three beds and the few pieces of clothing that we each owned. It was my job to help Mom pack the kitchen. The wood stove didn't belong to us so it stayed. We were told we wouldn't need one anyway. Having a place with a bathroom meant no outhouse. I couldn't imagine taking that! *(Laughing out loud)*. So the outhouse stayed! I did think it was neat that we would be getting a toilet like the ones at school. You could actually sit on those without falling in, which had often happened to me in the ten-gallon bucket. Sometimes my brothers had even pushed me in. It was not a pleasant experience! Shitty actually!!

Mom didn't say much as we packed away the few dishes and pots from the kitchen. She remained silent as we were driven to our new home. I kept asking questions as I always did. "What will the people be like there? Will our house be much different? Will we still be able to walk to school?"

"Just stop with all the questions," my father burst out as he slapped me across the back of the head. "You will see when you get there," he muttered.

I took that as my cue to be silent, like my mom. For the rest of the trip I sat quietly, soaking up all the splendour I saw through the window. To be seen and not heard. I was getting better at that. Liz had taught me how to be silent. But this was a different silence; it was forced.

When we finally arrived at our new house, it was nothing like I had imagined, nothing like our old house. It was a long row of ten apartments all stuck together. I had never seen houses like this before. There was nothing like this in Seal Rocks.

Our house was number ten. As I looked around I could see that there was a marsh behind us. This excited me at first, as I thought there would be bakeapples to pick in the summertime. Bakeapples were a survival food that my aunts and I would pick and sit and eat for hours at a time. To my dismay, I later discovered that this was not the case. No berries at all! The marsh was just a wet, soggy piece of property.

It was my father who opened the door to our new home and, with such arrogance, walked in first. The house felt awkward to me, but the others quickly took rein and ran straight up the stairs to see the rest of it. I plunked myself at the bottom of the stairs and stayed there for a long time with my knees to my chest and my arms folded around them. I felt claustrophobic, paralyzed even, as if I couldn't breathe.

STAIRS! THE THOUGHT OF STAIRS! There were stairs to the basement, stairs to the bedrooms! I felt a state of panic enter my body. I hated this new house already! I didn't care if it had running water, a fridge and a stove. I didn't care that we had a bathroom with a shower, a tub and a toilet. And I didn't care that my brothers and sisters and I now had our own rooms. All I was thinking about was how I was going to escape. I needed a place where I could run and hide. Looking around I could see there was none. I felt like a prisoner trapped in a cell. My mind and body were stricken with fear. I stayed in the corner of the stairs until he pushed me up to what was to become my new hell.

Define Yourself

Yes, we will all have some form of trauma in our life
We will all have our own way of responding to it
We will all do the best we can with the tools we have
We were built that way
Our trauma does not define who we are
It is our past
A perception as we see it in the now
And in the now we are never the same
Forever changing
So now we work on what we have at this moment
With love
Compassion
More love
And more compassion
Now we live and learn gracefully
Once we learn
That our trauma does not define who we are
We do.

Kellie JOYce – June 2013

Chapter Eighteen

It was time for all of us to get a tour of the new school and meet the principal. Because the school was a lengthy distance from where we lived, a bus picked us up across the road from the apartments. It didn't take long to figure out that our building was full of kids. I quickly learned that we were all in the same boat, welfare brats! That's what they called us at school. None of our parents worked. No jobs, no money, struggling to live day by day. We were being supported by welfare. I didn't really know what that meant, just that it was why we were ridiculed and why we were constant targets for the other kids who treated us as if we had a disease or something awful that nobody wanted to catch.

St. Joseph's was so much bigger than our old school. When we were introduced to the principal, we were given a warm welcome. He was a grey-haired man in a brown-striped suit and he wore a huge smile as he greeted me. "What a pleasure it is to welcome a student like you to our school, Miss Kellie. I wish all our students had a report card like yours." I was surprised by the principal's comments and took a liking to him right away. "Wow!" I thought. I never got praised this highly at home even though I was an A+ student. My parents never said anything about my grades. My home life was killing me, but I had shown great restraint at my other school by not telling anyone.

"Excuse me, sir," I interrupted. "Do you have a track team at your school?" My father's eyes pierced mine, showing his disapproval. But I continued what I was saying. "I am a good runner and would love to join."

"Indeed we do," the principal replied as he went on to tell me all about it and said that he thought I would make a great addition to the team. In my old school you weren't offered an opportunity like this until you reached grade eight. I felt excited for two reasons. First, I knew I could join the group and do something I was passionate about, and second, it was my new escape. I was smiling on the inside; however, I administered restraint in front of my parents.

One of the good things about my mom was that she encouraged us to get involved in whatever we could. At least, in whatever didn't cost. I didn't feel she did much else to support our growth in the outside world, but she tried her best to make sure that my father didn't prevent us from getting involved in the free activities.

I didn't waste any time. I joined the track team that very first day. Mr. Pollard, the coach, was also very welcoming. He informed me that the next practice would be in two days, right after school. I assured him I would be there. And I was.

I quickly bonded with Helen, one of the girls on the track team. She invited me to run with her so that she could show me the route.

"How long have you been running, Helen?" I asked.

"Since I began walking," she chuckled. "I have been on the track team since grade four, Kellie. How about you? How long have you been running?"

I felt sheepish telling her that this was my first time on a track team for fear that she would mock me. However I blurted out, "Well, this is my first time, Helen. I have always wanted to join but have never had the opportunity."

I waited for her to catch her breath as she replied, "WOW! Really? You're an awesome runner! No one at school could ever keep up with me, but I'll have a hard time beating you." I could see by her response that she was amazed. As we finished the practice Helen quickly gave me a hug and thanked me for running with her. I felt that I was the one who should be thanking her. She had made me feel accepted, as if I had always been part of the team.

"Nice to meet you, Kellie," she yelled back at me as we both headed home.

"See you next week," I echoed. I had made a new friend. I was thinking about Helen's kindness as I walked the long route back home. She and I hadn't really talked much as we ran, partly because of the overwhelming beauty that surrounded us and partly because of the feeling of contentment that comes over you when nature's face is shining on you. To me it felt like the path to healing. It reminded me once again of my times with Liz.

Chapter Nineteen

Running soon became my drug of choice. For my brother Claude, it was pot, alcohol and cigarettes. He smoked and drank even more now, but not me. I ran!

My Catholic family was really involved with the church. My parents allowed Claude to become a chauffeur for the Monseigneur of our new church. That meant he was gone a lot. The rest of us rarely got to see him. Every weekend the Monseigneur would take my brother away from everyone to his cabin in the woods. Claude would come home, high as a kite, with enough cigarettes to last him and my parents for the week.

Claude was very animated when he was stoned, but when he came down off his high, he never spoke a word or mentioned anything about what had taken place in the cabin in the woods. My parents didn't question him, yet Claude's silence bothered me. It seemed that my brother was not living, just existing. I tried talking to him. I tried to get him to laugh. I failed at both.

"What do I know?" I said to myself. Well, I knew he drove the Monseigneur's car without a license because he was too young to drive. I knew he was allowed to miss school whenever he wanted. I knew my brother, at thirteen years of age, was allowed to do drugs, drink and smoke, and my parents said nothing. I, however, was hardly allowed to leave the house. It was my job to roll my parents' cigarettes for the week. When my father put his head on my lap, I was forced to rub it for hours. Yes. To be seen and not heard, that is what was expected of me.

43

Chapter Twenty

It wasn't long after our move that Mom informed us that she would be going to Seal Rocks for the weekend. My Aunt Marlene was living with us at the time. Mom figured it would be okay for Aunt Marlene to take care of us while she went home to visit her family and friends. Mom took real good care of Dad before she left. She cooked him a roaster full of his favourite ribs, got him a bottle of rum and had sex with him before leaving. I guess she was trying to keep him happy and avoid another beating.

Not long after my mom had gone, my father drank most of the bottle of rum. He summoned my aunt to get me. Everyone did what my father said, everyone including me. My aunt grabbed me by the arm and dragged me to the front door. I could see my father's reflection in the window. "Get in here!" he said a few times, his voice getting louder each time. He quickly slammed the door behind me and locked it. As my father closed the drape that covered the window, I could see a sad look on my aunt's face.

"Up those stairs. NOW!" he yelled at me. I ran as fast as I could up to my room and lay on my bed in the fetal position. I could hear his footsteps as he slowly staggered up the stairs. When he entered my room he was coughing loudly and clearing his throat.

"GET UNDRESSED!" he demanded in a stern voice. I started to cry. He staggered toward me and all I could see was his huge stomach wiggling in front of my face. He grabbed me by the hair so tightly that I screamed. "Stop the fucking crying and screaming," he yelled as he placed his hand over my mouth to silence me. "Now get undressed," he said as he started to undo his own pants. I did what he said to do and I lay there without moving as my father raped my body and my soul.

"If you tell anyone, and I mean anyone, I will kill you, and your mother too. Do you hear?" he whispered in my ear when he had finished with me. I nodded my head yes, but no words would come out. As I wiped the tears that ran down my cheeks, I felt an emptiness that no words could describe. I felt dead inside.

I lay still as my father got dressed. He had a smirk on his face while doing so. "Go and get your sisters and bring them back home," he said as he left my room. When I returned with them he had gone to bed and was asleep.

I remained with my sisters for the rest of the night, but I couldn't sleep. I stayed awake the whole night until my mom came home the next day. I wanted to tell her, to let her know what he had done to me. But all I could hear was his voice saying he would kill her. So many times he had come close to doing just that. Sometimes he beat her so badly she couldn't walk. I was afraid for my mom's life, so I remained silent. My father just acted as if nothing had happened. I was deadened.

That was the start, the start of the control that he placed over me. I had always known that my mom feared my father, but now that he had raped me, I feared him as well. That fear grew as he continued to inflict abuse upon me. He was constantly grabbing me in my private parts, or pulling my hand to feel his privates. Sometimes he would sit on the toilet in the bathroom watching me as I bathed, and then he would fondle me. At other times when he and his men friends were drinking, he would leave them alone with Mom while he went upstairs to bed pretending he was going to sleep. Instead he would come into my room, dangle his penis in front of my face, and then stick it in my mouth.

"Lick it like a lollipop," he would say while my two sisters continued to sleep in the bed beside me.

I thought back to the day I had heard my mom having sex with her father. Was this what everyone did but nobody talked about? Maybe it was normal after all. If it was so wrong, why didn't my mom stop it? I really wanted answers, but I couldn't ask anyone. Who could I ask? None of my friends spoke of things like this happening. At eleven years of age there was nowhere to turn. I had so many questions, but so few answers. Nothing made sense and there was no one to explain things to me.

So I continued to do as I was told and said nothing. Mom kept going away every other weekend, while I kept going away in my head as he abused me. I had found solace in my place of words, where I could write stories and feel my presence in them. I had learned to do this well, so well in fact, that I didn't seem to care anymore. My writings allowed me to smile for the moment and not feel my actual pain.

Here He Comes

Please God, I pray
Don't let him enter our room tonight
He is naked again
Comes over to me
I move so he sees I'm awake
Allowing my sisters to play the pretend game
Of being asleep.

His huge cock dangles in my face
I hear him jerk off
As he cums he grabs my hand
To hold his cock
As it pulsates in my tiny hand
He pushes my head towards it
I let out a small whimper
"Shut the fuck up!"
He whispers in my ear
"Or I will kill you."

"Junior, Junior,"
I hear my mom calling to my dad
"Where are you?"
He pretends he is so drunk
That he went into the wrong room.

My sisters were spared once again
As my pain grew stronger
I wished he had killed me instead.
I prayed to God for that.

Kellie JOYce – February 1984

Chapter Twenty-One

I often amazed my teachers with my writing. At times I even amazed myself. No one believed me when I said I couldn't see pictures. "How can you write so well and not see the images?" one teacher asked. I couldn't explain. I couldn't tell her of the horror that was going on at home, that if I were able to see pictures, his face would be a constant torture. I was grateful for my gift of writing, and not seeing pictures in my head didn't bother me at all. So my internal writing, as well as the running, were places where I could escape and cause less damage to myself.

I learned that the busier I became the less time I had to think. So at school I became involved in every group I could. My grades were a different story. I had gone from an A+ student to a failing one. I remember how proud of me the principal had been when I met him. I felt awful for letting him down. I was going to have to repeat grade six.

My mom blamed my failure on our move. Maybe it helped her to remain blind to our reality. But I knew darn well why I had failed. My mind just didn't work the same anymore. My father's behaviour towards me had altered my thinking. I was on constant alert, always worried about what was going to happen next. I never really allowed myself to feel the stillness. I was not able to focus and remember the crap that I was being taught, especially in History class. I didn't want to learn facts about wars that had gone on years ago. I was in my own war, struggling to survive. Nobody cared about my battle!! So it was easy to see why my grades in History and other subjects dropped drastically.

Chapter Twenty-Two

Today I had to use the code again. When my father gets in one of his drunken states, beating my mom into the ground, I have to be very loud and bang on the wall to signal the neighbour to call the police.

The police take their sweet time getting to our house. To them, a call to our house is a regular occurrence, kind of like going home at the end of a shift. And, by the time they do arrive, the damage is done. Mom has already suffered at the hand and mouth of my father. Sometimes she would have also suffered other things, like a gun pointed at her head. She would tell us the gun was empty and we shouldn't worry. However, fear would be evident in her eyes. You see, my father was a hunter and bullets were kept not far from the gun.

When the police did arrive, nothing was ever done to him. He would be sent to bed and then the police would leave. My mom had once again become a victim of his sickness. Mom would try to reassure us all. She would even defend his behaviour. Boy, did that cause me to feel an anger I could not express! I felt so helpless, so out of control.

After a while Mom asked me to stop using the code. I obeyed her wishes as I saw no reason to continue its use.

Chapter Twenty-Three

I was beginning to understand more about the cycle of abuse at home. We had talked briefly about physical and sexual abuse in class. I went to a Catholic school, so when I say briefly, I mean briefly. We were still being taught that a woman was to obey her husband. Mom indeed did that, risking the protection of both herself and her children, likely because of the shame and guilt she felt. I wanted to ask questions so that the teacher would elaborate; yet I found the strength to refrain from asking. Instead I had an internal conversation with myself. I wasn't thinking like a kid. I was scheming of ways to protect my sisters from the horrors that took place at home. While most of my friends were building snowmen, playing ice hockey, skating and doing the things kids do, I was planning escape routes.

As I found myself becoming stronger, I began trying to identify who I was. Teenage years had shown an ugly face, and I believed I was having an identity crisis. I had developed a voice that I wanted others to hear. I was setting boundaries for myself.

I laugh at that as I write. Nobody in my family has any idea what that means.

I was about to take control and stand up to my father. This was the day I would test that out.

I asked my mom if I could join Air Cadets. She hadn't heard of it, so I explained in detail what it was all about. I told her about this friendly lady who came to our school and talked about the benefits of being part of such an incredible group. I told her that Air Cadets was free, and this was important if Mom was going to agree to my joining. The word 'free' caught her attention right away; however, my father acted as if he weren't listening, but I could see he was hanging off my every word.

"She said we could go to summer camp, Mom, and get paid. I would give you the money for food. I could learn to fly a plane, play sports, shoot photos and do such neat stuff. Please Mom, may I join?" I couldn't hide my excitement. Just knowing that I could do all of those things for free made me feel so emotional. I couldn't wait to join. "We have to go to sign up tonight, Mom. May I go? Please, please?" I was begging now.

"Of course, Kellie. You can join Air Cadets as long as it's okay with your father," my mom replied as she left to have evening tea with the neighbours.

I slowly walked over to where my father was sitting. "Well, can I, Dad? Can I join Air Cadets?"

"Come over here," he said, nodding his head and motioning me towards him. Walking hesitantly I felt my body begin to shiver. He extended his arm toward me and grabbed me by the front of my shirt. My father pulled me toward him and slid his rough hands down the front of my track pants, inserting his big round fingers between my legs and up inside of me. As he pushed his head to my face and stuck his tongue down my throat, moving his fingers in and out of my vagina, something frightening happened. My body started to tingle and shake, and a gush of wetness ran down my legs.

My father pulled his hand away more suddenly than usual. I felt he too was startled by what had just happened. I thought perhaps I was hurt or something, but the feeling was too good. I think I must have been in shock as he grabbed my tiny hand and put it in his, directing me to stroke his penis up and down until this white stuff came out. All the time he was moaning like I had heard him do many times when he was having sex with my mom. I wondered if what had just taken place was sex too. Then my father pushed me to the floor and said that I was blocking the TV. "You can go to Cadets now," I barely heard him say as I distanced myself from him, my mind in a muddle.

I quickly changed my clothes, and left to go and register. I was still trying to understand what had just happened to my body. This was not what I had in mind for boundaries. I had been planning to stand up to him and tell him to stop doing the things that made me feel yucky. I had mixed thoughts and feelings, but I said nothing.

It became evident there was no way of stopping this now. The more involved I became in Air Cadets, the more he exercised control over me. I said nothing and allowed him to abuse me over and over again. I thought about what my mom had often said to me. "Just listen to him and do what he says." So that's how I survived. I thought and acted like my mother. If I gave in to his demands, he would give me what I wanted. In this case, needed.

My wish was to remain in Cadets, so I allowed my father to do what he wanted to me, knowing now that the only place that I could escape from being abused was in my mind.

Where Would I Go

It was safe there

I saw nothing
I heard nothing
I felt numb
And allowed my body to be objectified

I didn't speak
Or move
But inside I cried

Nobody saw where I went

It wasn't a pretty field of flowers
Or a hot warm beach with sand
It was just a place of nothing
Every time that's where I would land

But it was safe there

Kellie JOYce – April 2012

Chapter Twenty-Four

The uniform we wore at Air Cadets meant so much to me. It was the finest piece of clothing I had ever owned. I was shown how to care for it. I used to borrow my neighbour's iron once a week to make sure the creases were well pressed and could be seen during inspection. We were given black boots to polish and spit shine. I spent hours on those boots and they shone so that you could almost see the reflection of your teeth in them.

In Air Cadets we were all treated the same. We were shown respect. Until now I had not known what that felt like. We were given equal opportunities to achieve growth on many levels. I am guessing that many of us ended up in Air Cadets for the same reasons. There was no cost involved and it was a great place to escape and experience new things.

During my five years as a Cadet I learned so much. I learned how people with different personalities interacted with one another, how to problem solve and how to work as a team. I learned about friendships and relationships, respect, honour and love. I learned about opportunity and the world. I began to see my own character develop now that I was away from the turmoil of life at home. I discovered how outgoing, fun and energetic I was. My peers would comment on my great sense of humour and my big heart. I started to laugh and to have fun. This was all so foreign to me. Overwhelming at times.

My mom insisted that my grades improve or else she would remove me from Air Cadets. I once again became a star pupil and remained a member of my squadron. I dove into everything that the 807 Air Cadets offered. I was a member of the Drill Team, the Photography Club, the Shooting Club (even though I hated guns!), sports groups, camping groups and even the fashion club. I excelled in photography and it was here that my passion grew. In my second year of Cadets, I received an award for top photographer. As I was more of a tomboy, I didn't really enjoy the fashion club. Still I used it more for 'female bonding'. I always had a difficult time connecting with women because I enjoyed men a lot more.

Today that surprises me as I was being betrayed daily by the one man I should have been able to trust and love, my father. I had tried really hard to gain control over my own sexual identity, and, in so doing, fight my father in his efforts to destroy it. I had sworn that I would excel in this area and continue fighting until I won the battle. I'm still fighting it today.

Cadets allowed me to be away from the house almost every evening. Unfortunately this allowed my father to use me more often as well. As long as I did what he said, I was free to go. Sometimes I gave into his demands just to find out he had no intention of letting me go to my group. There was no doubt that my father controlled my every move. Until, that is, I was selected to go to Air Cadet Camp in Greenwood, Nova Scotia. I battled as to whether or not I should go. I worried about the implications my leaving would have on my younger siblings. Would my father turn to abusing them while I was away? Mom was not traveling to Seal Rocks very much anymore so I tried to rationalize in my mind that they would be safe from him while I was away. So I left for camp. I later discovered that my father had been sexually abusing my sisters long before that.

The following year I was chosen to do a six-week paid training for Physical Fitness and Recreational Training (P&RT). I was allowed to go on the basis that I would send the money home to my parents for food. I agreed to do just that and set off on one of the most rewarding adventures of my life.

It was here that I met Tom, another Newfoundlander who came from Lewisport, and we connected right away. We were taking different courses but I got to spend many evenings alone with him. Besides Charlie, who was my Air Cadet friend back home, no boy had ever shown me attention. I found myself thinking that this was love and one evening, after dark, I had sex with Tom under one of the big trees on the base. He told me that he had had sex many times before and he assumed that I had as well. I did not correct him.

I was excited as I returned to my barracks to wash my bloody underwear in the sink. I thought I was getting my period as I was now fifteen and my period had still not begun. But it was a false alarm. To me it didn't matter that Tom might have just used me for sex. I was giddy inside knowing that someone other than my father could make my body respond this way. I wanted to share my excitement with someone, but I thought it best to keep quiet. I couldn't tell anyone what was happening at home either. The writing in my head had stopped for a while, but that summer, in Base Borden, Ontario, I had changed. I knew that when I returned home things were going to be different for me.

Chapter Twenty-Five

When I returned to Cadets in September of that year, having successfully completed the Fitness course, I was announced as being the weekly evening instructor for the other Cadets in my squadron. I would be instructing at our local public gym so Charlie and I would get to spend more time together. We were already really good friends, and, on occasion, he would kiss me. Charlie was the first boy that I had ever kissed.

One cold and snowy afternoon as we sat in the snow bank during our lunch break, Charlie put his arms around my waist and pulled me close to him. He gently kissed me on the lips and that was it, the day we made it official. We were boyfriend and girlfriend. I wasn't really sure what that meant for the two of us. I don't think he knew either, but, as all our friends were pairing up, we too were now 'an item'.

Charlie became someone I could trust, someone in whom I could confide. We were inseparable. We started to hang out at school and at Cadets. I even joined the Math Club that he belonged to. How ironic, as I sucked at Math and was flunking it. All the members of the club were exceptionally smart and were friends of Charlie. Everyone liked him. He was so kind and compassionate. The more time I spent with him, the more I liked him, and eventually I came to love him.

This boy was forcing me to ask myself a lot of questions. My head and my body were so confused. At first Charlie had no idea what was happening to me at home. I felt too embarrassed to tell him. So for a while I didn't, but soon felt I had no choice. It angered Charlie to hear such degrading stories. From that point on, with Charlie's support, I began to consider finding a way out.

Dynamics at home had really started to change. Mom was beginning to realize how happy and fulfilling Cadets made me feel. She started to stand up for me when I was begging my father to let me go to Cadets. You see, by now, I had stopped giving in to my father and I wouldn't even let him touch me. This made him very angry. Of course, if it were at night when the choice was between my younger sisters or me, I would allow myself to bear the burden of my father's sickness. I would tell them to turn their heads and pretend they were sleeping.

It was then that the physical beatings started. My father found every excuse to beat me with the belt or his fist. I would go to school with broken glasses, held together by tape, and with bruises on my body. The kids would just laugh at me, make jokes and taunt me even more.

For many years I thought I was doing right by staying home and not sharing with anyone the hidden tortures that I was enduring, the daily physical, sexual and, eventually, emotional traumas. I convinced myself that it wasn't all that bad. Mom dealt with a lot more I thought, so I put up and shut up, just like he said. But the day finally came when something or someone had to change. I knew it would be someone and it had to be me. I had to find a way to escape from the emotional prison in which I was living. It was killing me!

Silence

The slow Killer
*   That   Knocks*
*   Kindly to*
*   Knight the*
*   Knave.*

Kellie JOYce – April 2012

Chapter Twenty-Six

My father was beginning to lose the control he had over me. His desperation grew, as did his anger. One Sunday my father demanded that I go to church. It seems he had discovered, by opening a personal letter, that, while at summer camp, I had had sex with Tom. I refused to go. "I want you to go and rid yourself of all your sins," he said to me. This day he physically dragged me through the streets of our town of Corner Brook. It became a huge public display as he roughly pulled me by my hair. I was screaming and yelling. I didn't care who saw us. And yes, everyone was looking. I felt so humiliated. I wanted to die. I even tried to pull myself into the traffic as a car came toward us. But he just yanked my hair even harder, bringing me to my knees in pain.

"Next week I'll buy you a leash, my little doggie," he said, laughing at me as I lay crying on the ground. Those words, I felt, were some of the cruelest he ever to spoke to me. He treated our dog better than me. That was a harsh reality for me to accept. I knew there would be no next week for me, but I whispered not a word.

My father, the hypocrite, made me go inside the church and he just stood there smirking. I went inside, knelt at my pew and talked to God while he waited for me outside until the service was over. I said to him the whole way home.

I acted like a good little girl and obeyed everything he said that day. I felt that he had rubbed it in my face by letting me know that he was still the one in control. I made up my mind. I couldn't survive in this environment any longer. I had thought that by doing what my father asked, I had been protecting my sisters. But I had discovered he hadn't spared them. A few months ago I had walked in on him with my sister Jessy. It was then I knew that I needed help to get them out of the house. I thought that if I told someone, my sisters would eventually be safe from more of his abuse. I made up my mind. I was going to expose the secrets that went on in our house, and I did.

Chapter Twenty-Seven

Mom usually stayed in bed every morning until we went off to school. Today I asked her to get up. At first she resisted. "I'm not coming home today, Mom," I blurted out. My father had gone off into the woods to go fishing so it was easy for Mom and I to talk freely. Mom quickly got dressed and followed me downstairs.

"What do you mean, you're not coming home today, Kellie? Where you gonna go?"

In a quiet voice, almost plaintively begging her to listen, the words sadly rolled off my lips. "Mom, I don't know, but I'm not coming home. I can't take this anymore!"

"Kellie, you're only gonna make things worse. Don't be silly. I'll see you this evening."

In the same sad tone I replied, "No, Mom, you won't see me this evening." I took a quick look around and headed for the bus stop where my other siblings were already waiting. I got on the bus and it was there that I came up with a plan.

When I got to school Charlie was waiting for me, like he always was. I told him what had happened the day before and that I had had enough. He supported my decision and tried to reassure me that I was doing the right thing.

The bell for class rang, yet today I didn't go to class. Instead I went straight to the Guidance Counselor's office. The door was open, so I walked right in and sat there waiting for the counselor to see me. Charlie said he had spoken with Mr. Rogers many times and that I had no reason to fear him. If I needed help, Charlie often told me, this was the place to go. I hoped he was right.

I could tell Mr. Rogers was surprised to see me sitting there. "Well, hello there," he said, reaching out to shake my hand. "And who might you be?"

"Hello, Mr. Rogers. My name is Kellie. Kellie Garnier, and I came here because I never want to go home again. And if you make me, I will run away."

"May I close the door so we can talk about it?" he asked. I nodded my head yes. I didn't hold back. I told him everything and made it quite clear that I never wanted to go back home again. Mr. Rogers asked me all kinds of questions and I answered them all. He showed compassion and understanding for what I was telling him. Charlie was right! Mr. Rogers explained what he would like to do to help me. I knew what he meant when he said he would have to get Children's Aid involved because they were the people who had deemed our home in Seal Rocks unfit. They were the people who were responsible for our move to Corner Brook, but I didn't care. Mr. Rogers left his office to make the call and get my siblings out of class. Within half an hour both a police officer and a social worker from Children's Aid were at the school questioning us. Like always, my brother, Steven, said very little; however, my two younger sisters confirmed my story to the authorities.

All the while I could hear my mom's words over and over in my head. "You're gonna make things worse, Kellie. You're gonna make things worse."

Kellie JOYce

I didn't care because I didn't think things could get any worse. By now my brain was racing. A series of thoughts kept cycling thought my head.

I thought I had been protecting my sisters. I thought my father wouldn't turn to them if I did what he asked.

I thought my mother already had enough with which to deal. If she could endure so much pain and abuse, why couldn't I?

I thought by saying nothing I was being 'STRONG'. At least that's how Mom made it seem.

It was for these reasons that I had stayed at home for so long. Over the last few weeks I had come to realize that none of these were valid reasons. Now I had nothing to hold me back so I had told Mr. Rogers about the abuse in the hope that we would all be safe.

It had taken until I was fifteen to stand up to my father. It was then that I told him I had endured enough of his shit. I declared that I was somebody who mattered and that I too deserved to be happy and loved. I didn't really believe that at the time, but I had taken the first step and I knew I had to try to find happiness.

Mr. Rogers didn't really go into the consequences of my disclosure. I was naive as to what would really happen, but I do remember the teenager in me thinking I knew it all. As I observe the life of my teenage daughters today, I can imagine what that might look like, and I laugh out loud. I write now from the mind of a forty-five year old. Reflecting back, I remember the tension that was released from my body when I finally told someone what my father was doing to me and to my sisters. Sharing the fear of what I was living with lessened my burden a great deal, but it did not prepare me for the events that followed.

The authorities went to our home and immediately removed my father. He was charged and put in jail until his bail was set. Mom appeared shocked to learn what was happening. At first she said she believed my sisters and me, but that quickly changed. Her fear of him and what he might do to her, I guess, was what changed her mind.

The next day he was back home.

Chapter Twenty-Eight

I was placed with one of my mom's sisters and her family for the first little while. That didn't work out very well. My uncle was a good friend of my father, in fact his only friend, so he didn't want to believe that my father was capable of the things I had accused him of doing. At this point, that's all it was, an accusation. It was my word against his. My uncle, fearing that I would accuse him and his buddies of doing the same things that I said my father had done, made sure he closed my bedroom door when his friends came over to play poker and have a few drinks. "We don't want to be accused of anything we didn't do," he would sarcastically remark.

I had shared my uncle's behaviour with my aunt and that was enough to make her confess. For the first time she shared with her husband the abuse that she had endured from her own father. Just like what had been happening to me, it seems my mom's dad had been abusing not only my mom, but also her siblings. After my uncle learned this, he tried to be nicer to me. He now understood, from his own wife's pain, that I could be telling the truth. I hold a deep respect for my Aunt Elizabeth. By sharing her story with her husband she had made me realize, in some small way, that she believed me. Yet I knew I couldn't stay there any longer.

Delores, Charlie's sister, said I could stay with her for a while until Lindsay, my social worker, found me a new foster home. By this time Charlie and I had developed a deep and intimate relationship. Living with his sister made it extremely easy for us to see each other. Delores had two boys, aged five and seven. I became very close to them because Charlie and I would quite frequently babysit them.

Charlie and I talked of marriage, of having children of our own some day. Over time Charlie taught me that I was capable of love. He taught me the importance of touching and being touched. When we had our intimate moments alone he would make love to me. My body would be reminded of the things that my father did to me. The pleasure and pain were so connected. It seemed that the more emotional the pain, the greater the pleasure. I would often cry, but my crying allowed the pain to be released. Those were moments of healing.

Charlie was so loving and understanding. He often asked me if I wanted him to stop. "Please don't. It is important for my healing," I would tell him.

Looking back now I understand how an orgasm and its intensity were related to my emotional self. Pleasure plus pain equates to orgasm; that's what my body had learned and how it responded.

Charlie was in his last year of high school and was preparing to go off to military college. I didn't want him to go. I selfishly wanted him to stay with me, marry me and have a family. Of course that didn't happen. And even worse, after he left, I discovered that his family didn't approve of me. I remember telling his mom and sister of our plans to marry. His mom had laughed a bit, a nervous laughter. "Don't be silly," she had said. "You are just kids. Charlie will find himself a good wife one day. You won't be marrying him. Military College will change all that." I took that to mean that I was not good enough for her son. My father's words, "You're a nobody, you don't matter, no one will ever have you," popped in and out of my head.

After that it didn't seem right that I stay at Charlie's sister's place. I didn't feel good about staying with a family that didn't love or approve of me. So I asked my social worker, Lindsay, to find me a new foster home as quickly as possible. Still, I wanted Charlie to know how proud I was of him and how his love had kept me strong even when he wasn't physically present. Later on I attended his graduation from Military College, but I never told him of the conversation I had had with his mother and his sister.

Today Charlie still holds a special spot in my heart. The love we shared has never died.

Discarded

We see it in nature all the time
Mothers having to leave their young
Abandoned
And I try to rationalize it
To help me feel less of a
Discarded human being

Helpless
Homeless
Worthless

A human being
Without a purpose
Just an empty shell
Walking about
Deadened by my reality

Discarded
Left to rot

Kellie JOYce – December 1984

Chapter Twenty-Nine

In the meantime, during Charlie's absence, I was dealing with the aftermath of my confessions. Life at school was one of suffering and torment. The guidance counselor and teachers were at a loss as to how to handle my anger. The realization of how very alone I was in the world hit me like a ton of bricks. By telling the truth I had alienated everyone: my parents, my siblings, but most importantly, the boy I loved. I had lost Charlie, and was lost without him. My anger spiraled and my need for control surfaced. My sexuality became an outlet and I allowed the boys, but mostly men, to get close enough to fall in love with me. Then I would bolt. Men became my targets, as if I was playing a game and I was the hunter. I wanted to pierce their hearts, to hurt them, and then let them go to suffer in the pain of abandonment. I used the tools that my mother taught me, and I felt that I excelled at it.

This went on for about a year awaiting trial. Jason, Cecil, Rodney, Derek...fudge, there were so many of them.

I wasn't hurting them. I was hurting myself by allowing them to use me. I see that clearly now.

Chapter Thirty

It was the night before I had to face my father in court. He had driven by my foster home in his car numerous times trying to intimidate me. My brother Claude had chased after me with a knife, trying, in his drunken and stoned state, to kill me. My siblings at school had cursed and spit at me for what I was doing. My mom was the only one I had not seen the day before trial.

Around two o'clock in the morning I decided to walk the streets of Corner Brook. I was alone in my thoughts, thinking of the events that would take place the next day. I found myself standing on top of a bridge that night. "You're not gonna jump are you?" I heard a soft voice behind me ask. It was Serge, a young French native whom I had met the week before at a Cadet dance. He was from another part of the Island and was attending college.

I looked into his eyes and smiled. "No, I would probably only get a few broken bones and skinned knees. Please help me down." I chuckled as he extended his hand to take mine.

Serge walked me home and came inside to make sure I was safe. And yes, we had sex. Sex was love to me back then.

I now know that this is not true. I had allowed myself to believe it then. Since that's what I always saw, it was natural that I should think that. It has taken me twenty-five years to undo those thoughts and realize that sex is not love after all. It is merely an act. Sex can mean nothing.

Chapter Thirty-One

Serge gave me the emotional support for the events that took place the next day. But what guided me, what carried me, was the love Charlie had for me in his heart.

My father stood before a judge and jury to be tried for the things he had done to me. He never took the stand to defend himself. I was the one on the stand for hours and hours, answering one question after another. It felt as if I were the one on trial.

My father just sat there with a quirky grin on his face as he watched me. I was having a hard time, knowing that my decision to stand up to him was causing everyone so much pain. At this point I really didn't care so much about my own pain. My sisters kept yelling out, "Please don't take my daddy away," and I too begged the jury not to take him away. Back when I had first approached the guidance counselor, I was convinced that I was prepared to do anything to help my family and remove them from harm. I hadn't anticipated the emotional pain that a trial would cause and the impact it would have on my siblings. I was torn between their pain and what I knew was right.

The judge spoke directly to me that day. "Kellie, you are a strong young woman. You have done nothing wrong. You have shown much strength and wisdom. I know it's not what you wish, but we have to send your father away. He is the adult here. He needs to be accountable for what he has done to you. Do you understand? If not now, you will one day. You know what is right and doing the right thing will guide you like it has here today. I wish you all the best in the future. It has been a pleasure to have you in my courtroom."

I needed someone in authority to say those things to me. Throughout the year, while awaiting the trial, no one had believed me except my social worker, Lindsay. I also knew it was her job to believe me. That day in the courtroom my mother was not there to support me. I felt so abandoned by her. But she wasn't there to support my father either. That spoke volumes. Throughout the trial it was Lindsay who continually reassured me. I realize that I did have my mother there. Only it was Lindsay who had taken her place.

When the guilty verdict was announced, my brother called me a 'fucking home wrecker'. My father was taken away to serve his sentence, and it was then that his attorney tried speaking to me. "I'm sorry," she said, weeping. "I'm sorry for doing what I had to do to you on that stand."

"How could you?" I fired back. "How could you defend someone you know is guilty?"

At seventeen, I didn't understand her role. Today I do. We are all deemed innocent until proven guilty. My father had the right to a fair trial. I didn't believe the lawyer's tears that day, but now, as I write, and as my own tears saturate the page, I do believe her. Experiencing the pain of sharing my story through the eyes of an adult and not those of that fearful little girl, I believe her. I, too, would have tried to console that hurt and abandoned child.

A thought made me happy that day. My mom was now free for the next two years, and so were my sisters. No more daily beatings, no more abuse. I left the courtroom, content in that knowledge.

But I also knew, one day, he would darken our door once more. He would come back, throw his weight around and destroy what was left of our fragile, shattered family.

Perhaps those twelve jurors were not aware of the full impact of their decision that day. As hard as it was to see my family torn apart, a family with whom I no longer had contact, I needed to hear that verdict. For the first time in a long time, life would become bearable. Someone had believed me. That day I found the strength to value life and start living again.

The guilty verdict saved my life!

The Court Case

For each little word spoken
My heart bled
For each answer
The tears I shed

As I sat among the jurors
Swore to tell the truth
I detested every moment
The charges not wanting to pursue

But now realizing
It was far from too late
I went and told everything
Leaving my heart with hate

The people intensely listened
As if they really cared
They sat silently in their chairs
As our stories were being shared

But as my story
Was slowly being told
I could sense the surroundings
Feeling empty and so cold

Puzzled minds once entered the room
But now they seemed so sure
And as they left one by one
I was the last to shut the door

Kellie JOYce

As I walked away
To a new beginning of my life
I knew I would never forget
Those moments that felt like
The stabbing of a knife

And I was right
I never did.

Kellie JOYce – November 1988

Chapter Thirty-Two

I felt so alone after the trial. Everyone told me that the family was grieving the loss of my father. I thought that I had done them a favour, but it seemed no one else saw it that way. At school the guidance counselor and the teachers remained at a loss as to how to cope with me and deal with my anger. My siblings treated me like an outsider. They would still curse and say mean things to me when they passed me in the halls between classes. It felt like I was constantly on fire, being burned. The pain hurt that much. I just wanted to be out of there. And putting my brother and me in the same class, how cruel was that? I often wondered who was responsible for that.

Chapter Thirty-Three

In spite of everything the year flew by and Christmas was rapidly approaching. I usually spent the holidays with my family and friends, but now I had no one. I had pushed everyone away. The only people I had allowed into my life were the ones who used me. I knew that this Christmas would be exceptionally hard.

I had been placed in foster care with a Jehovah's Witness family. Patricia was a single mom with two young children. She had a daughter named Tracey who was around the same age as my youngest sister. I could see that Tracey accepted me and looked up to me. She would often come to me for advice and ask how to deal with boy problems. I wasn't convinced that I was the right one to ask; however, she often told me I had been helpful. In a way, it made me feel like part of a family. I had never felt like that with my own siblings, although I had longed to feel that sense of belonging.

Tracey's brother, Andrew, was a few years younger than she was, but he hardly spoke to me. We never connected the way his sister and I did. I felt that he was lonely and that he too was missing a father figure in his life. I could relate to that; moreover, I could relate to missing my whole family.

However, I didn't spend Christmas with Patricia and her family. Instead I accepted an invitation to go to Serge's. He lived in a remote part of the island, far away from Corner Brook, and for that reason it was good that I went.

Serge and I tried to have an intimate relationship that

night. It was no use. I ended up calling out Charlie's name as we had sex on the back of the Ski-Doo that was parked in his father's shed. He took it well. In fact, he told me that he had come into my life for a purpose. He was adamant in saying that he was sent to me by God, to help me through this rough time in my life. He had a lot more faith than I did. Nevertheless, he was there for me when I needed a friend. I told him I would always be grateful for that.

The next day, Boxing Day, I returned to my foster home. I got to see Charlie one last time while he was home for the holidays. We spent a few hours passing the time doing what we often did. He read to me as I lay in his lap. I found comfort in that. I still hear his voice in my head. That day was the last time we were together.

I don't remember much of the months that followed. I do remember I continued my role as an active member of the 807 Air Cadets. I became squadron commander and took home numerous awards that year. Most of the time I disassociated and continued to follow a path of abuse towards myself and towards the men who pretended to care.

Looking back, as I reflect on what it was like to have no father figure in my life, I realize why I was so drawn to older men. I found them attractive and alluring. I felt I could look up to them and love and be loved. But I was just trying to recreate the loving and trusting bond that I was missing.

Throughout my childhood there were many father figures. Ray was the first. He was one of Mom's lovers. I admired him and we developed a close relationship. This was the first time I dreamed of another man being my father. Not having one of my own to respect, I felt that Ray could take his place. The first time he disappointed me, I let go of that fantasy and continued my search.

During my days in Air Cadets I met Brian who became father figure number two. I was seventeen and he was forty-four. He had sex with me many times and I felt as if he loved me. I soon realized I was just a joy toy that he used and abused.

Then came Rodney. He was number three. I visited him almost every evening in his brother's gym where he practised weight training. I became one of his weights until he grew bored and discarded me.

At Cadet camp Norman became my fourth father figure. He set the bar high when it came to lovemaking. No one could reach his heights. Still, I kept searching. This pattern continued while I dealt with the negative effects of the trial. The loss of my family and my need for love grew. This led me to meet Andre who lived two doors down from my foster home.

Andre was in his late fifties. He was a pleasant, grey-haired man with a smile that could light up a room. He was soft spoken, tender, caring, kind and thoughtful. He was everything my father wasn't. Andre and I quickly became good friends. He would pick me up from school. Most days we would go for long drives and or take walks together. That year his wife, Grace, spent a lot of time visiting her mom in Prince Edward Island, and Andre and I got to spend many hours together. We became really close friends. Andre worked at the airport and he would often bring me the leftover meals from the planes. This food was much better than what I was eating at my foster home. Bob, Patricia's friend, would often drop off outdated food from the local grocery store, food that really should have been thrown in the dump. We never got physically sick, but I always felt sick having to eat it. I remember how excited Patricia would be, but Tracey and I were not impressed. We would make crazy faces to show our disproval, yet we ate the food and looked past our disgust.

I couldn't say no to the nights when Andre would wine and dine me after he finished work. I couldn't say no to the great meals, the awesome company and the lavish gifts. Despite the fact that Lindsay had warned me to be careful and stay away from Andre, I didn't listen. I wanted someone to love and someone to love me. I felt that Andre loved me, but eventually I discovered I was merely an obsession.

I didn't realize it then, but I see it clearly now.

And I couldn't understand why Grace was getting angrier and angrier with me.

Today I get it. Andre wanted me for the same reason all the other men wanted me. For sex!!

Chapter Thirty-Four

Andre wanted me to come to his place for Christmas, but Grace still continued to resent me. "You're gonna have to meet my oldest son, Kellie. He will be coming home from Toronto for the holidays," Andre said. It was evident that he was trying to find a way to have me join their family for Christmas dinner.

When his son returned home, Andre convinced him that there was a really nice young woman a few doors down that he should meet.

On Christmas Eve there was a knock at the door. "Go and answer it, Kellie," I remember Tracey whispering. "I have no idea who is there, but, boy, is he cute!" she giggled. I opened the door and there he was. Les.

A tiny young man with salt and pepper hair looked directly into my eyes and said, "Hi. I'm Les, Andre's son, and he sent me over to meet a lovely young lady." He put out his hand to shake mine.

"Yes, that would be me," I replied as I looked into his eyes. It was love at first sight!

"Andre never told me how handsome you were," I piped up.

"Oh, he told me how beautiful you were, and he was right," Les said, smiling at me. "Wanna go for a walk to the beach?" he asked. I could hear Tracey laughing around the corner.

"Sure, I would love that," I answered as I grabbed my winter coat and boots and headed out the door. Les held my hand right away. It felt natural. It felt like home.

We walked and talked for hours. He took me downtown and bought me a pair of earrings for Christmas. I let him pick them out. They were in the shape of a bell. "Just ring the bell whenever you need me and I'll come running," Les said jokingly. Right from the start I loved his sense of humour.

I went to his parents' home for Christmas dinner the next evening, despite his mother's disapproval. Now it seemed as if his father and his younger brother, Derek, did not approve of me either. That didn't matter. I just wanted to be with Les. And, for the few days he was home from Ontario, we spent every waking minute together.

That long list of names of those who had used me in the past included both Les' father and his brother. Les had told me of the conversation he had had with his brother before coming over to meet me. "If you want an easy lay, that's the girl for you," his brother had said. I remembered an evening after a party when his brother had invited me over to his place. We had ended up having sex and then he had shipped me home in a taxi. I had not realized it had been Les' brother until I went to Andre's house and saw a picture of his family.

I guess there were plenty of men that I had forgotten, but I couldn't forget Les. This was the first time I had spent so much time with a man and not had sex with him. I knew then that this relationship was going to be different.

I felt different. I was surprised that Les had enough confidence in me to tell me of his brother's conversation, but maybe that's why we didn't sleep together the first time we met. His brother was right. I would have been an easy lay, but Les didn't want to use or abuse me. He respected me from the start, despite what he had been told.

I could tell that Andre was not impressed that Les and I had connected so well. He wanted things to be the same between us after Les went back to Ontario, but they never were. It was only then that I truly understood how sick and unhealthy Andre's intentions towards me were. Lindsay was right. I should have trusted her.

In the four months that followed Les and I grew even closer. We would talk for hours on the phone. I wrote to him every day and he replied to many of my letters. Because of his job with Air Canada he was often able to visit me for a few days at a time. I had found the kind of love that I had shared with Charlie, one of passion, emotional connection and trust. I felt that my relationship with Les was going to be like that and even more.

Wings of Love

He has flown into my life unexpectedly
Perched restlessly at my side
He has spread his feathers
Over my heart
Yet not covering all ground
We stand still
To the possibilities
Of one day
Flying away together
Gracefully.

Kellie JOYce - December 1985

Chapter Thirty-Five

Grasping at straws I went in search of the only family member I knew that had no connection to my immediate family. That was my grandfather, my father's father. My grandparents had divorced when my father was a baby, so he never knew his father. At first my grandfather was very appreciative and supportive towards our meeting. In fact, he offered to pay my way to Ontario. I graciously accepted for two reasons. First, Les had agreed to meet me at the airport and drive me there. And second, finally I might have found someone I could once again call family. Both these thoughts brought me much happiness.

When I arrived, it didn't take me long to find my grandfather. He lived in the small town of Napanee, which is just outside of Kingston. I really enjoyed my first visit with him. Mind you, in the beginning, it was really difficult to look at him as my father looked so much like him. Once I got past the physical resemblance I began talking. My grandfather answered my questions and showed me a lot of family pictures.

During my stay I met several of his friends and they all seemed genuinely happy to meet me. I noticed that my grandfather drank a lot, just like my father. However, that first meeting left me feeling hopeful. I returned to Newfoundland leaving behind the two newest and most important people in my life.

Chapter Thirty-Six

Les and I continued to correspond and this brought us even closer. We still had not taken our relationship to one of physical intimacy. Although there had been many opportunities, Les had never taken advantage of them. I was baffled. This was a first for me. I would later find out that there would be many firsts with Les.

My grandfather paid for a second visit to Ontario. I got to witness the real side of him during this visit, but, more importantly, I also got to see another side of Les.

Once again Les picked me up at the airport and took me back to his place. But this time it was very different. I was greeted with roses when I stepped off the plane. There were roses in the car, at the door and on the balcony. He had hidden roses everywhere. He seemed so passionate and at every opportunity he would pull out a rose and hand it to me, saying, "I love you, Kel."

The last rose was the most special as it was left on the pillow of his bed where, for the first time, we made love. This was not like all the other times. Making love to Les was as if I had finally found myself whole. I had had many more physical experiences than Les, but none of them compared to the level of intimacy we shared that night. Perhaps the chemistry was heightened because he was seven years older than I and he was looking for someone to complete him. I felt like this was my first 'woman' moment. Inside I was still a kid, but that night I experienced a taste of adulthood. For much of my childhood I had played the role of an adult, but now I actually felt like one.

I didn't want this feeling to end, and I could tell that Les didn't either. Making love to Les made it possible to feel like this, so why would I want it to end? I didn't! Our bodies had become one, our minds were in sync with one another and our souls were forever connected.

I hated to leave, but the next day Les drove the four hours to take me to Napanee to see my grandfather. My grandfather answered the door and we could see he was quite tipsy. Les wasn't sure whether he should leave me, but I reassured him that I would be okay. It was hard to kiss Les goodbye, but I wanted so much to have some connection with blood family.

I trusted my grandfather, but that trust soon vanished. I was in the shower when my grandfather pushed open the door to 'use the bathroom'. He lived in a seniors' lodge and there were no locks on bathroom doors. At first I thought this seemed innocent enough, but he soon proved me wrong. I waited behind the curtain for him to leave but he just continued to stand there. "Shut the door behind you, Grandpa," I called out. Instead he peeked behind the curtain and said, "I want to do the same thing to you as your father did."

Flashbacks flooded my mind. "GET OUT!! GET OUT!" I yelled over and over until he finally left. I guess he knew someone would eventually hear me. Quickly I finished my shower, dressed, packed my bag and left. I went a few doors down the hall to Richard's, one of Grandpa's friends I had met on the first visit. I told him what had happened and asked to use his telephone. I called Les, who had just gone to bed, and asked him to come and get me. He was shocked, and told me he was on his way.

My hope of a relationship with a family member had been shattered. I found solace in Les' arms. He was the one person in the whole world I felt I could trust. I spent a whole week with him. Our time together was like something I had never before known or experienced. I hated the thought of going back home, of returning to school, of trying to finish my math credits, of dealing with my angry siblings and all my losses. But I did go back.

Chapter Thirty-Seven

I had only been home for about a week when I got the invitation. It was as an early birthday present from Les, a one-way ticket to Ontario. At this point in my life it was my way out, away from this town, foster care, school, Newfoundland and all the hurtful memories. More important though, it held the promise of love, possibly marriage, and a chance to have a real family of my own.

I accepted without hesitation and left for Ontario a week before my nineteenth birthday. I told my foster family my great news. The only other person I told was Andre. He begged me to remain in Newfoundland and start a life with him. He declared his love for me and even said that he would leave Grace for me.

"Andre, I'm going to Ontario to start a life with your son. I love him, not you. We are just friends." I tried to make him understand that I loved him only as a friend. I was thinking that if Les knew how his father felt it would break his heart. So I vowed to say nothing. I said good-bye to Andre and away I went, but he didn't let it end there.

It wasn't all roses with Les like I had imagined it would be. I had a hard time adjusting to the fast pace of life in Ontario, to Keith, the roommate, and to finding a job that I liked. And, oh yeah. The drugs. Les hadn't told me that he and Keith used daily. That's how often they did it. Having seen what it had done to my brother, I was terrified of pot use and would go out at night, even though it was late, to avoid being around them. Eventually Les would come searching for me, only to find me behind one of the bushes on the apartment property curled up in a ball, like a scared little child. I had left my body and gone to a place in my mind where I felt safe with my words.

It took me a while but I eventually told him I had had enough. Keith moved out and Les and I moved to a smaller apartment. As time went on, I got to learn more and more about Les. Although I thought we shared everything together, I learned, much later, that this was not true. In the beginning I felt we had no secrets from each other. So yes, I did end up telling him about his father and me. I had to, because his father kept coming up and spending time at our place. That left me alone with Andre while Les was at work. Les' dad continued to try and convince me to move back to Newfoundland to be with him.

This went on for the first year, so that was why I had to tell Les. I knew it would affect my friendship with Andre, but I had to come clean with his son. I was glad I did. It made us closer. As I had predicted, Andre turned against me and hardly ever spoke to me again. After that, whenever he and his wife came to Ontario, they stayed with one of Andre's sisters and would just come for a brief visit with us. Those visits were stressful for both of us, but it allowed Les to visit with his mother whom he loved dearly.

Over time I got to know Les' mom a lot better and realized that things Andre had told me about her were untrue. He had lied so he could try to get closer to me. Grace was battling depression and this worried Les. We often talked about how cruelly Andre treated her and felt that this, in part, contributed to her depression. I felt awful for the pain I had caused her.

Today I realize that I was just a child at the time and it was Andre who had taken advantage of me. However, I am so grateful that I met Andre for he brought me to Les. He gave me the gift of love, his son.

Chapter Thirty-Eight

The following year I was working as a manager at a local store and earning a decent wage. Back then eleven dollars an hour for retail was a respectable salary. Les and I had decided to tackle the debts he owed. His drug use was slowly decreasing so less money was being spent for this habit. I knew he still did pot, but never at home. I guess I was sort of okay with this, but not really. As long as he used when I wasn't around, it was 'somewhat' alright. Not totally, but bearable.

Les was climbing the ladder at his work and new job opportunities were arising. He talked about applying for a job as a baggage agent. I encouraged him to try as it meant more money and better hours. It also meant I would have the opportunity to put a bug in his ear about my wanting to get married and start a family. We had been together for more than two years now and I needed more than he was giving.

I remember the conversation so vividly, probably because I was the only one talking. "Les, it's me or the drugs. It's marriage or I walk. I want to start a family of my own, have kids and I want to be with a man who wants that too."

Les never said a word, just got dressed for work. I thought for sure that my ultimatum had destroyed any chance of a life with this man I loved. He didn't call me from work like he usually did every evening. Actually, he often called several times in an evening. My mind was racing and not with the most pleasant of thoughts. I couldn't imagine a life without Les. I had allowed him into my heart, just as I had Charlie, and I knew that he too would always hold a special place there.

I was asleep that night when he arrived home from work. I couldn't believe my eyes when I awoke the next morning. I saw a few unopened bottles of alcohol on the counter, a fridge full of my favourite foods and, sitting on the coffee table, a dozen of the most beautiful yellow roses I had ever seen and a typewriter.

A very animated Les said, "Good morning, sweetheart. I have great news! Come here and sit with me. I have been offered a new position and I just need to pass a typing test to get the job. Wanna see how well I can type already? I practised all night. Oh, and sorry I didn't call. I was preoccupied."

"Sure, hon," I answered. I had never seen Les this way. It was kind of strange at first, until he started to type and then it all made sense.

"Read it, Kel," he said.

Kellie, will you marry me????? That's all he had typed.

"That's great, hon," I replied, not really looking at the typed words. "You're doing great."

"No. No. Read it out loud, Kellie," and his voice got louder.

"Ok. Ok. I'll read it." At this point I did not understand. So, he could type. Big deal! Kellie, will you marry me????? I read out loud. And then a bell went off. "You mean for real?" My mouth opened wide and I stared straight at him. He nodded his head yes.

"Well, type your answer," Les said, moving aside so I could type an answer to his proposal. I proudly typed the word Yes and he hugged me and held me close. We spent so much of that day celebrating our love, crying together in our happiness and sharing our dreams of being together forever. I felt as if this were a dream come true. I was actually going to be Les' wife! "Kellie JOYce. That has a nice ring to it," I told him.

He bent over, put his head close to mine and whispered in my ear, "I know it's silly, but I believe." And we both burst out laughing. I felt like that little girl in 'Miracle on 34th Street'. If you wish for something long enough, it just might happen.

Chapter Thirty-Nine

That was early in December. We planned to have the wedding a few months later on Valentine's Day. Les told me he didn't want to waste any more time and I agreed. I remember calling Charlie to tell him the news. He was happy for me and wished me much love and happiness. I was really hoping for his approval. He still held a huge part of my heart, but I knew it was time to let go and start my new life with Les. I felt that I was finally ready to do that.

Most weddings are about elaborate dresses, expensive food, fancy tables and huge crowds, but not ours. Our wedding was going to be one of LOVE. Les and I wanted to make sure that this day was not one of financial ruin or of unwanted stress, so plans for the wedding were kept to a minimum. We decided to rent the hall in the apartment building where we lived. A few co-workers and I decorated it. I covered the wall with poetry I had written as part of my wedding gift to Les. I made all the food myself and put a small stereo in the corner so we would have music for dancing. Our guest list was short. It included a few of my co-workers, Maxine, my girlfriend from one of my foster homes who happened to be living in Toronto now and, of course, Les' family.

I asked Andre to walk me down the aisle because I had no one else to ask. It was an awkward moment for him, but, because I was marrying his son, he said he would. Les' brother was asked to be the best man. That was awkward for him too, but not for Les and me. We knew nothing would affect us that day.

On February 14th, 1989, Valentine's Day, we were wed. Les drove with his aunts to Mississauga City Hall. Upon arriving, the aunts told him the building looked like a prison. We joked about their comments later that evening. I was fortunate enough to be driven in a limousine, a wedding gift from a cousin. The driver drove around for an extra half hour, making me late for my own wedding. The Justice of the Peace almost cancelled the service. As he performed the ceremony, he spoke so quickly he could have been saying anything. Les and I laughed, but the others were all in a panic. The ceremony lasted no more than fifteen minutes. We were now officially husband and wife. I took Les' surname, JOYce, and rejoiced in throwing away the name Garnier. I was so proud to be Les' wife. Nothing could possibly destroy the love and happiness I felt that day.

I briefly thought of my mom; however, I knew I had to bury those thoughts so as not to spoil our special day. There was not a happier event in my life to date than my wedding day. The day in the courtroom when the judge read the guilty verdict came close, but marrying Les topped even that. Now I really knew what love and happiness were, and, on this day, our wedding day, I revelled in those feelings.

It was time for our first dance as husband and wife. Les let me choose the song. Anne Murray had always been a favourite of mine, so I chose 'Could I Have This Dance'. I thought this was the most appropriate song to begin our life together. As we danced we cried because we both could relate to the words 'for the rest of my life'. I snuggled into his shoulder, not caring if anyone saw my tears. I only wanted to feel close to my husband. It felt so perfect. I wanted the dance to last forever, just like it did in the words of the song. I knew with all certainty that I had chosen a partner with whom I wanted to spend the rest of my life. I knew I had married my soul mate.

Les and I didn't even make love on our wedding night. Instead we stayed awake in our Montreal hotel room, eating junk food, pigging out on all the snacks that were stocked in the mini fridge in our room. Then we laughed and laughed when we saw the enormous bill at checkout. We thought that the snacks were free with the room. Instead it cost us seventy-six dollars! In total the bill for the room was two hundred dollars. We thought this was insane! But it was a night to remember for sure.

That only ever happened once. We had learned that food and drinks found in a mini fridge in a hotel room were not free. In years to come we would often tell that story to our friends. They would laugh at our ignorance.

Chapter Forty

I felt like the happiest woman in the world; however, my longing to be part of a bigger family unit did not change. I thought that being married to Les would erase the need to have my family in my life, but it didn't. Marriage did lessen my desire somewhat, but the need was still great, so I sought therapy to help me cope with the loss. I didn't want this burden I carried to affect the life I had with my new husband.

I had learned that my father had been released from prison and was back home with Mom. I felt it was time to contact my childhood social worker, Lindsay. We had remained connected even though I had moved to Ontario. My therapist thought that I was ready to confront my abuser. I was no longer that scared little child; I was a stronger adult ready to have that conversation. I wanted to hear what my father had to say for himself. That day in the courtroom I had wanted him to say something, to feel something for what he had done to me, but he had said nothing. Instead I remember him sitting there with that smirk on his face. I felt as if he were laughing at me like always, only in court he did it silently to save face. It had hurt me just the same, and now it was time to allow him the opportunity to answer the questions I had for him after all these years. A part of me hoped that my father and I could get beyond the hurt and pain that affected our relationship. I hoped we could start over and build trust again. I desperately wanted my parents to be a part of the family that I hoped to soon start. In my heart I felt the chance of resolving the past was slim, but I decided to try one last time before shutting that door. I also knew I wanted Lindsay to be part of that meeting.

My boss was very understanding of the situation and was kind enough to give me some time off work so I could fly home to Newfoundland. She demonstrated both compassion and support and told me to take all the time I needed.

I had arranged to meet Lindsay at her work. She drove me to the place where my father would be during lunch hour. It had been easy to find him. He was working on yet another welfare project. He and the workers were outside eating their lunches when I approached him. I walked straight over to my father even though I could see that telltale smirk on his face. He looked like a fragile old man to me now, but I could still sense that fearful little girl in me begin to tense up. The closer I got to him, the more aware I became of my fear. I tried really hard not to show it. "This should be so simple," I said to myself. "I just have to ask him why?" I engaged in some self-talk before the actual words came out.

"Why did you do what you did to me, Dad?" I asked in a very non-confrontational way. He responded with the same facial expression he had used in the courtroom, followed by a huge outburst of laughter. This did not really surprise me, but still it hurt deeply.

"Don't you realize you have robbed yourself of a loving relationship with your daughter and any future grandchildren? Don't you care? You will never be a part of my life or my family again. I will never allow you to hurt me or anyone I love!" I said all this then waited. I waited for him to respond, to react verbally, but he said nothing. He just kept laughing as I sadly walked away. Finally I felt that I had the closure I needed. I hadn't spoken directly to him that day in the courtroom, but this day I was in control. I had given my father an opportunity to make things right and to help me understand, but he had chosen instead to laugh.

Lindsay put her arm around my waist as we both walked back to her car. "I'm proud of you, girl," she said. That's all I needed to hear as we drove off.

That day I divorced my father. I knew that we would never have a healthy relationship and that his sickness was something I no longer had to allow as part of my life. Unfortunately, it also meant a lot more. I would have to divorce my biological mother as well. I wasn't ready to make that decision in my head or in my heart. I still hoped that someday my mom and I would be able to have a relationship. As for my father, although he was very much alive, for me he was now dead.

It was time to say good-bye to Lindsay. We had talked a bit about my mom and her fragile state of existence. She knew I longed to have a relationship with her. She hugged me tightly and said, "Don't give up on her, Kel. One day, when he is gone and she is no longer fearful of him and his threats, you could have your mother back in your life." I cried knowing that was very unlikely, but I did find some comfort in the thought. I hoped she was right. I told Lindsay how much I appreciated her and that she was a better mom to me than mine had ever been. It was a sad reality, but the truth.

I had completed what I came to do in Newfoundland. It was time to go home. The next day I went back to Ontario to be with my husband and start a family of our own.

Chapter Forty-One

Dealing with the reality of losing my family was more challenging to my psyche than I thought it would be. I became severely depressed. I had to stop working. While Les worked longer and longer hours in order to pay the bills, I fell deeper and deeper into an abyss. I lost all interest in life and people. Photography, which once had brought me much comfort, now held no interest.

Les had never seen this side of me before and was at a loss as to how to deal with the situation. He ended up taking me to the emergency room at our local hospital. Based on my symptoms the doctor on call diagnosed me as having severe depression and gave me a prescription that he said would help me to 'think straight'. There was no way I wanted to take drugs in order to cope. I had fought to be in control all my life. When I told the doctor I would refuse to take any medication, he said, on that basis, he would not admit me for treatment and sent me home.

Looking back now, I realize how out of control I really was. Maybe there were benefits to taking medication and maybe my recovery would have happened sooner. Yet despite this, I am grateful for choosing the path I did.

In my mind I felt only shame and the stigma of helplessness. But I was convinced that I was strong enough to cope without the aid of medications or doctors. It took me about six months to get back to being my old self. During this time my boss continued to be very supportive and, because she valued my hard work ethic, I was eventually able to return to work. Once again I began writing, doing my photography, cooking and enjoying all the things life has to offer. Les had been so good to me throughout this whole ordeal. I really felt his love for me. I was confident that I had made the right choice by making him my lifelong partner.

Chapter Forty-Two

At twenty-one my one real dream was to be a mom. To be clear, this was the only dream that I felt I could really accomplish. I had so much to prove to my own mom. Yes, I wanted to be a writer or maybe a psychologist, but in my head I could still hear those negative thoughts. "You're a nobody. You will never be successful." And no matter how hard I tried to drown them out, those thoughts remained in my head. Sadly, for much of my life, I had believed those thoughts.

Since I knew my father couldn't destroy my dream, I was determined that I would become a mom. But I didn't want to be just any mom. I wanted to be a mother of girls, girls that I could call my own and of whom I could be proud. I wanted to prove that I would be the good mom that mine never was. I never spoke aloud about my dream, but it often consumed my thoughts.

Les and I wasted no time trying to start a family. It was so much fun. For me, having a baby was my primary focus, but for Les, his focus was on me. He would often tell me that kids would be wonderful, but, if it were just he and I, that would be fine. He felt he could live his whole life with no kids.

Every day my husband made me feel like the happiest woman in the world. He made sure we celebrated every moment we shared together. For the next five years Les and I lived and played like two frolicking kittens. We were happy in our own little world. I felt as if Les were a part of me. We were so connected that our friends would often comment that it made them sick to see us together.

When we were together I loved to cook gourmet meals. Les would arrive home in the wee small hours of the morning and we would eat by candlelight, laughing and enjoying each other's company. Together we spent quite a lot of time travelling and exploring new places. For me, the only thing missing in our life was a child.

Finally, after five long years of dreaming and waiting, Les and I were told we were going to be parents. Our years of playing had paid off. We learned we were going to be parents of not just one baby, rather parents of two babies. I was expecting twins! I knew twins ran in my family because my grandmother had had twins. I felt happier than ever. Regrettably, that feeling didn't last long.

Four months into the pregnancy we noticed that I wasn't getting any bigger and some of the earlier signs of pregnancy were gone. At first I thought this was normal, but I wasn't gaining weight at all. In fact, I was losing weight. I weighed one hundred and twelve pounds and was four months pregnant. It was when I started spotting that we decided to go and see a doctor. We went to the hospital and the doctor insisted I have a vaginal ultrasound. At that moment I knew something was very wrong. Because I was suspicious of the doctor's diagnosis, he suggested I call my own doctor to confirm that this was a normal and necessary procedure. He handed me the telephone and I called him. After my doctor confirmed that this was indeed normal and necessary I allowed the doctor to continue with the tests.

The doctor inserted a long probe with what looked like a condom on the end into my vagina and this test confirmed what he already knew. Our hopes of having a

Kellie JOYce

family were destroyed. It seemed that, because of my
blood type, my body had rejected the twins. I was given a
needle and told that this would prevent the same thing
from happening the next time, if there were a next time.
The doctor said that the fetuses would just release
themselves over the next couple of weeks. Then I was
sent home. I was devastated!

The next day Les and I went to our family doctor who was
angered by the way I had been treated at the emergency
room. He admitted me to the hospital for a D&C, a
procedure that would remove anything left over from the
pregnancy. Knowing that the bits and pieces coming out
of me could have been my babies was torture and I was
relieved that the decision to have this done was made by
my doctor and not by me.

*To this day I appreciate how my family doctor helped me to
cope with this great loss in my life.*

Chapter Forty-Three

The months that followed were difficult and I felt another bout of depression setting in. Yet this time I knew what I was dealing with and that it was quite normal to feel this way after such a loss. My worry was not as great as the first time I had experienced depression. But this didn't stop Les and me from trying even harder. The doctor had said that if I had conceived once, it could happen again. However, after two years of trying and having no success, our family doctor decided to send us to a fertility specialist. By now I was twenty-seven years old and I was desperate to have a baby.

Les insisted that I quit my job and take a vacation. He felt that the stress of focusing on having a baby would lessen if we went away. We booked a trip to Germany. My brother, Steven, who was in the military, was stationed there. We decided we would look him up.

I hadn't seen my brother since high school so I wasn't sure what to expect. When we reunited it was as if we had never parted. There was no talk of our dysfunctional childhood. In fact, my brother had actually described a great childhood to his girlfriend when he learned we were planning to come and visit him. I felt somewhat angered by this. It was as if we had grown up in different households. Perhaps that was his way of dealing with the past. Denial is bliss, so they say.

Steven's behaviour added a little stress to our trip, but Les and I were determined to let nothing bother us. Together with my brother and his girlfriend we explored the beautiful countryside of the Black Forest and Lahr. It was so lush and green there. During one of our daytime excursions, a truck carrying oil had spilled its load and I remember how the people who lived there were so devastated. Government officials, who spoke no English, became involved. The driver of the oil truck was a black American who spoke no German. Les tried talking with him to give him some emotional support, but to no avail. So Kirsten, Steven's girlfriend, offered her services as an interpreter. She tried to diffuse the German officials who were being really harsh. She explained that the Black Forest was a protected environment. This was bad news for the truck driver. He would be required to spend a lot of money to clean up the spill. Eventually an officer who spoke English arrived at the scene, so we continued on our way.

We experienced everything from climbing mountains to climbing apple trees. We sat in the open fields and enjoyed the freshness of the clean air. The taste of the fresh fruit bursting with juice felt as if we were experiencing the eating of an apple for the first time. It was delectable.

We loved the fact that all the businesses closed during the lunch hour and everyone went home to have lunch with their families. This day at Kristen's house it was spaghetti with sauce for lunch. Les and I were surprised when the women of the house took off their tops, revealing their bras, and sat there eating their spaghetti. This German custom did not bother us at all, but we chose to keep out shirts on. All in all it was a great vacation and I got to see and share another part of the world with Les.

The plane ride home was brutal. Back then smoking was

permitted on all flights. I spent eleven hours with a blanket over my head to try to filter out the sickening smell of the smoke that filled the air. We were so relieved when we finally landed in Toronto. The air was not nearly as fresh as it had been in Germany. However, it was much better than being locked inside a plane unable to escape those deadly fumes.

Les' parents had stayed in our apartment while we were away. They greeted us upon our arrival and told us that we had won a Jeep. In order to accept the Jeep, the promoters of the contest required the winner to pose for a photo for the local newspaper. Since Les and his dad shared the same surname it was easy for his dad to pose on our behalf. We thought it was the funniest thing ever and we chuckled when we heard this. We were filled with excitement and couldn't wait to see our new Jeep.

We opened the front door of our apartment and there it was. Our Jeep was a motorized toy! Back then a toy like this for kids was the cat's meow. But we weren't kids and had no use for it. So we decided to leave it under Les' cousin's Christmas tree as a present from Santa. A real Jeep would have been nice though, I thought to myself.

Chapter Forty-Four

The next day we were anxiously awaiting our appointment with the fertility specialist. We were ready to begin treatment and start a family. The specialist was a short, petite East Indian man. He was so pleasant and upbeat. We told him about the complications we had experienced and he said that I should start taking fertility pills right away. One of his last questions surprised me. "And how have you been feeling lately, Kellie? How is your mental state?"

I immediately replied, "Great, but I'm awfully tired and, come to think of it, my stomach is a little upset. I feel as if I may be coming down with the flu or something. We just got back from a trip to Germany so that might explain it."

Smiling, he looked right at me and asked, "You couldn't be pregnant, could you?"

"No doc, that's highly unlikely, but I can't be a hundred percent sure after all," I answered, rolling my eyes. "Our trip was very relaxing."

"Well, I need to be certain you aren't pregnant before I give you a prescription," he replied and he left the room. He came back shortly with a nurse who took a blood sample. Within ten minutes the doctor, wearing the biggest smile I had ever seen on such a small man said, "Congratulations! You're going to be parents. This is the quickest I have ever helped someone get pregnant." He laughed loudly, but Les and I just sat there numb and in shock.

I couldn't have been happier, but Les had a blank look on his face that puzzled me. After we left the office I asked if he was all right. "Aren't you excited, my love, about the news?"

"Kel, of course I am, but, to be honest, I'm afraid that things between us will change." Les had spoken very softly.

"Don't be silly," I said. "As I have always told you, nothing or anyone will ever come between us." I was not yet a mom, so I was still naive enough to think that a child would not come first on my list of priorities.

For the next six months I was so busy trying to get the baby's room in order. It was an exciting adventure searching for a crib, a dresser, a carriage and baby necessities. I was indeed overcompensating and going all out to make sure that our baby had the best of everything. Les didn't offer much input, so I chose most of what was needed. And, in my mind, it was okay that I was the one in control and making the decisions. It was my kind of high.

I started to notice some oddness in Les' behaviour. His emotional state was growing weaker and weaker. Les' mental health worried me a lot; however, the new life growing inside of me kept my mind busy and my spirits upbeat. Although I didn't choose to, I became Les' caregiver and I gladly assumed that role.

The nursery was finished and fit for a queen. The solid bleached hardwood furniture was stained a light colour. A brass daybed with a white patterned cover trimmed with lace stood in one corner of the room. It would be used when I needed to be close by for the night feedings. Green floral curtains, made using the new sewing machine I had received from Les at Christmas, hung freely but could be tied back to allow the light to shine through. The room was filled with the plush toys and hand knit blankets that had been given to our unborn child from friends who had attended my baby shower. Since an earlier ultrasound had determined that I was going to have a girl, the gifts were pink and frilly. I loved it! I loved the fact that my baby girl was going to have the best of everything.

Chapter Forty-Five

At a time in our lives when we had just about everything we had ever wanted or dreamed of, my world once again started to fall apart. Les was coming down with many odd illnesses. He was acting out of sorts and seemed very withdrawn. At first I thought it was due to the pregnancy, but I soon realized it was much more than that. Les started to develop a fear of people and situations. He wanted to be alone with me all the time. I tried to encourage him to spend some time doing his artwork, but he showed no interest in that whatsoever. Eventually his illness necessitated that he stop working. That meant we would be together all the time.

Finally I got some insight into what was going on and I began to understand. I learned that, for the last few months of my pregnancy, I had been dealing with the onset of my husband's severe mental illness. He had been diagnosed with Bipolar Disorder.

In retrospect, I didn't know how being diagnosed with a mental illness could affect the mind. I wish I had been more knowledgeable then. If so, I might have handled things differently.

At that time I knew little of the turmoil through which my husband was going. Les didn't speak much. Since I was so caught up with the magnificent human being growing inside of me, I didn't notice that he was silently struggling just to exist day by day. He didn't want me to tell a soul about what was happening. Because I wanted to honour his wishes and allow him some dignity, I too remained silent.

Chapter Forty-Six

During the latter part of my pregnancy, the doctor was keeping a close eye on me. About three weeks before my due date I had another ultrasound. My doctor was called. You know that silence when you are certain that something is going south? Well, this was one of those times.

The doctor reassured me that, although everything was okay with the baby, he was going to have to admit me and deliver the baby early. The office was just minutes from the hospital, so off we went and I was admitted. Our baby's arrival was imminent.

The doctor broke my water to speed up labour. There was a brief moment of excruciating pain as he put his fist inside of me and broke the lining that was protecting my baby. I sighed in relief as the warm water gushed down my inner thighs and made a puddle on the floor. It was at that moment that I demanded an epidural. I was not up for any more pain. The doctor ordered it and luckily the person who was to administer the epidural was at the hospital. I was given one right away. This was one of the scariest moments of my life. I was told to roll over onto my stomach and was reminded that it was important that I not move. I was given a long list of things that could go wrong if I did. I already hated needles but when I saw the long needle that had to be inserted into the base of my spine, my body was stricken with fear. I didn't want any more pain so I sat still and tried to be brave. The doctor then went away, saying he would check on me in a few hours. Les also left and said that he would come back later with my personal belongings.

The doctor assumed it would be about six to twelve hours before delivery. My fear and anxiety was through the roof. I was ready for the delivery now because the epidural had kicked in within the hour. I was totally numb and I felt very relaxed. The nurse informed me that my baby had stopped feeding, so that was why an early delivery was necessary. My baby was hooked up to a fetal heart monitor and watched closely. I now had to wait to become fully dilated. Less than half an hour later I felt pressure in my pelvic area. I reached down and I could feel what I thought was the head of the baby. I called for the nurse and explained my concern. "No, my love," she said. "It can't be the baby already. We just gave you an epidural and that should slow things down a little."

"I think you'd better check," I insisted.

"Well, we'll have a look," she said to ease my mind. By the look on her face, I knew. Holding her hand out flat like a stop sign, she said, "Don't push!" Within minutes three nurses surrounded my bed and were calling to see if the doctor was still in the building. I was lucky because he was there making his rounds. A nurse gave me the phone to call my husband.

It seemed so strange when Les said that he had had a few beers and needed to get someone to drive him back to the hospital. That was odd behaviour as he rarely drank. Perhaps he was not ready to be a father. No one was ready for this baby but I was. I was really ready and my excitement was obvious!

The nurses were running around like chickens with their

heads cut off, trying to prep for my baby's delivery. I was now totally dilated and this baby was ready to be born. I recall one of the nurses fearfully saying, "If the doc doesn't come soon we are going to have to deliver this baby without him!"

Les and the doctor arrived at the same time. Everything happened so fast. The doctor said I should stop talking and laughing and concentrate. Two pushes and our new baby girl began crying at the top of her lungs. Les got to cut the umbilical cord and was the first to hold her.

This moment lingers in my body making it impossible to forget even today.

The nurses cleaned the baby up and then Les handed me our little bundle of joy. "Here is Sarah," he lovingly said. "Kel, she is just as beautiful as her mom." For quite some time I basked in a moment of spiritual delight. Finally I had a daughter. I was a mom. Wow! This was my dream come true! Tears rolled down my cheeks as I kissed my baby for the first time. I felt an indescribable joy, something I had never experienced before. The moment was too wonderful for words. In disbelief I repeated over and over again that I was a mom. It had taken eight years for this moment to arrive, and as I put our daughter to my breast to feed her, I felt an instant bond. Shortly after the feeding she was placed under a lamp because she was a little jaundiced, having been born three weeks early. She was right next to my bed, so she did not leave my side. I watched her as she slept while Les and I held each other tight.

Sarah weighed five pounds and twelve ounces and was

born on December 21st, 1995.   Everything went off without a hitch with Sarah. She was just a few hours old and I could already sense the commitment in my heart to this helpless, loveable being. It was as if my world had changed in an instant.

Chapter Forty-Seven

By now Les was acting even stranger. He was not as overjoyed as I was. I could see fear in his eyes and his anxiety level had escalated. He continued to get sicker and sicker, and shortly after we took our bundle of joy home, he ended up in the psychiatric ward at one of the local hospitals. Les had taken an overdose of pills in an attempt to end his life. He later explained that it was a cry for help. He said he didn't want to die. He just wanted some help dealing with everything that was happening to him.

What should have been our first Christmas together as a family was spent with Les in the psych ward trying to get the help that he needed to deal with his mental illness. I, too, was changing and things were starting to happen to me that couldn't be explained. Physical things! I didn't have time to focus on myself and for a little while I tried to ignore them. Dealing with a newborn and a mentally ill husband took much of my energy. I found that it was getting more difficult to hold Sarah and to breast feed her. My energy level was at an all-time low and physically I had difficulty walking. The whole left side of my body was going numb. At first I was scared, thinking this was an after effect of the epidural. I sought medical advice from many different specialists who presented various scenarios, one of which was MS, Multiple Sclerosis. I couldn't concentrate on what I was hearing as I was thinking solely of my husband. I wanted the healthy Les back. I wanted him to share in my excitement of the family we had created. But I couldn't see an end in sight. Les' mental illness meant he was on long term disability.

I constantly feared that he might end his life. During those first six months he tried at least half a dozen times. I continued to try and keep strong for Sarah's sake. I did everything I could possibly do to keep my husband safe. Meanwhile, my own health was deteriorating and this caused me to go back and forth to neurologists to try to find solutions.

Ever since Les had become sick, our sex life had been put on the back burner. Despite this I was thinking about a sibling for Sarah. I really wanted her to have a little sister. A brother would be okay, but my preference was to have another girl. We had not been sexually active since that first day in the specialist's office when we were told that we had a chance to be parents again.

One day, although I knew I was asking a lot of him at the time, I begged Les to make love to me. I remember that day so vividly. "Please, Les. Please make love to me. I believe I'm ovulating and now would be a perfect time to conceive," I told him. "Make love to me so Sarah can have a sibling. If anything ever happened to you, I don't want her to be alone in the world."

Les did agree. But it was merely a physical act as there was no emotion in our lovemaking. The medications that had been prescribed for Les had removed most of his desire for intimacy and sexual fulfillment. The times when we would make love two or three times a day no longer existed. That took a toll on both of us.

For the next half hour I lay there with both my legs elevated. I knew that day that we had conceived a baby. Maybe because I wanted it so badly, I convinced myself that I felt it occurring right at that moment. I'm sure I did feel it happen. Three weeks later I went to a doctor and a blood test confirmed that baby number two was on the way. I remember the time, place and day this baby was conceived because it was the one and only time during this phase of our lives that Les and I had had sex.

Chapter Forty-Eight

Perhaps many would say this was a blessing from God, but at this time anything related to God caused me to doubt Him. I questioned whether He even existed at all. I wanted to ask Him why all this was happening to my husband and me. How could God be so cruel? On the other hand, I felt blessed that this baby inside of me was going to be a playmate for Sarah. Between all the pain and doubt, this pregnancy was the one thing I felt could give me the strength I needed and hope for the future.

Each day held the constant fear of what Les might do next. He was still somewhat in denial about his illness and would start and stop taking his prescribed medications. For a while I bought him some new art canvases and paints but he showed absolutely no interest in being creative again at this time. All my efforts to think of ideas that would help him find meaning and purpose once again in his life failed. I was really at a loss as to how to help him.

This year, being pregnant with our second child, was the most trying and difficult year of our marriage. Most of it passed in a blur. I can recall the daily struggles to take care of Sarah's needs and prepare for baby number two while watching Les as closely as I could. It was a struggle to get out of bed every day and difficult to walk, but I did because I was the one who had to make sure everyone's needs were met. I was the caretaker, caring for them, but ignoring my own physical symptoms that were worsening with each day that passed. Finally, because my daily life was being greatly impacted, I had to admit that I needed help.

Chapter Forty-Nine

I suspected that the baby I was carrying was going to be a girl, and, indeed, the ultrasound confirmed this. We also learned that our second child was going to be born soon. I was excited but, at the same time, fearful. I knew that the demands of taking care of two babies who would be only thirteen months apart in age would be almost entirely mine. I wanted a second child but thinking of the responsibility I would have to bear alone left me feeling overwhelmed.

Les continued to spend all his time at home as he was still not working. Our financial situation was worsening as we were only receiving sixty percent of his pay. That added even more pressure to our lives.

Sophia Deanna didn't give me much warning the day she came into the world. By the time I got to the hospital I was already fully dilated. A nurse examined me and said that the doctor had been called and was on his way. I was refused an epidural even though huge bold print on my chart read 'THIS PATIENT IS AUTHORIZED TO HAVE AN EPIDURAL UPON BEING ADMITTED TO HOSPITAL'.

"We can't give you an epidural, my love, or it will stop your labour," the nurse said. I begged but it was no use. My baby was ready to be born now.

For the next seven minutes I experienced the most excruciating pain I have ever felt, but then, there she was. Daughter number two! People often say that you forget the pain of childbirth. This is not my truth. I will never forget the pain I felt the day my beautiful daughter was born. It was as if my lower body were on fire. But it was worth it. That experience was something I will never forget!

Unfortunately the delivery had taken its toll on my already weakened body. In a very short time I became almost totally numb and I found it hard to hold my new baby close to my breast in order to feed her. The nurses helped by propping pillows under me.

Les had not actively participated in this delivery. Instead he had chosen to wait in the hall with Sarah until our baby was born. Although I had wanted him there with me, I was okay with his decision knowing that he was not in a good place at the time. When Les and Sarah finally came into the birthing room to see the new addition, neither of them seemed very pleased. I knew Sarah didn't really understand and so she wasn't sure what to make of this new bundle of joy. It took Les quite some time before he would hold her. I watched him closely as by now his attention span was not great. I remembered the times Les had been able to focus when he was painting a miniature watercolour using a single-haired paintbrush. Now he could barely hold our daughter for more than a few minutes.

My stay in the hospital was brief because I wanted to get back home to be with Sarah, Les and our new baby. Having Les' mom there was truly a blessing. I don't think I could have managed without her help.

Chapter Fifty

I couldn't totally relate to the emotions a man must feel when he loses his job, his mental state, his control, his talents, his feelings, the desire to want to live, in fact everything that identifies who he is. But I was becoming more and more aware that these losses were greatly affecting my husband.

On days when it was quiet in our house and both babies were having their late afternoon naps, Les and I would enjoy doing the dishes together as it gave us an opportunity to talk. It was on one of those days that Les, in a very calm and loving voice, said, "I think we would all be better off dead, Kel." Not sure that I had heard him correctly I asked him to repeat what he had said. "I believe we would all be better off dead, my love," he replied a second time. He continued by saying, "I am God, you know. I'm here to save us all from evil, from our pain and suffering. And those Americans, they're especially evil, you know. Kel, I have been thinking of a way to do away with all of us."

I stopped my husband at that moment, grabbed him by the arm, brought him into our living room and asked him to sit with me. With a big lump in my throat, I explained how fearful I felt listening to what he had just said. He remained convinced that the right thing to do was to kill all of us. I knew that the right thing to do was to go and talk to our doctor ASAP. Les agreed to go with me, but he wasn't about to change the way he felt.

Les' mom was out, so I called Kathy, our neighbour and friend, to come and watch the girls for us. I held Les' hand and walked across the road to the medical building. It was convenient having the medical building close by, and we were in luck as, on this particular afternoon, our family doctor was on call. As soon as I told the receptionist what had happened she took us to see the doctor right away. My doctor responded quickly. He closed his office and directed all the patients who were waiting to see him to go to the hospital instead. Then he called an ambulance and the three of us were taken to the hospital. Les was placed on a 'form one'. This meant he was a threat to himself and his family. He was sedated and the doctor began to look for an available place where he could send Les to receive the treatment he needed.

I don't know where I found the strength to be strong and calm through all of this, but I did. I loved my husband and despite everything he had said, I wanted to believe that he would never hurt us. Yet the numerous attempts to take his life left both doubt and fear in my mind.

Chapter Fifty-One

Les was hospitalized for three weeks and while he was there he was told that he would have to go to the Clarke Institute for further evaluation. This tormented him greatly and it became a daily ordeal to face his constant fear. He turned into a recluse and spoke to no one, not even me.

When he returned home we sat down in our living room and I could not see into the eyes or into the soul of this man before me. Where had my husband gone? "I need to know how you're feeling and what you're thinking, Les, so I can help you cope with the changes in our life. Please start writing to me daily to help me understand."

"Ok, Kel. I will try," he answered. I held my husband close and kissed him softly on the forehead.

"Thanks Les. That's all I can ask. I feel it really will help us." He picked up the morning paper and said he would start writing the next day.

Les kept his promise and the next day when we returned from the mall, he wrote these words to me.

Wed. Sept. 10, 1997

Hello Kellie:
My first letter to you – First off I wish to say that I enjoyed our trip to Square One– it was spontaneous and I liked the freedom of Sarah and I having lunch while you and Sophia shopped. That was a nice

compromise in the way of trust.

When I am thinking more clearly I realize what an obnoxious asshole I can be at times. Short tempered, arrogant, aggressive, mean of tongue.

And when I am clear in my thoughts I don't know what comes over me. Is it the medication or the lack of it. Is it my condition. Is it the anticipation of going to see the folks at the Clarke. Is it the realization that they may tell me my condition is irreversible and so am I lashing out in anger and frustration at the unknown. Is it the lack of sleep−lack of intimate relations −the sense of aloneness, as at times I feel I have already loss you as you struggle to keep your sanity and care for our two daughters. Is it some resentment in knowing that I do not always have control of my faculties and will have to grudgingly allow you to supervise my activities with our kids. And because of that the loss of my feelings of self worth as a parent and a person. Is it the sense of dissatisfaction in myself in never before having the strength to deal with the real issues that have plagued my life and my unwillingness to let anyone in. And how pissed off that now that I have opened up and bared my soul to all the morbid feelings and obsessions that I have bottled up inside I have in fact driven people further away and am even more alone. And

I am putting great distance between us and it is all or at least mostly all my fault for being so unwilling to open up. I hope I have not irreparably damaged our marriage and that if through these letters I can communicate to you what I am feeling and that if I can accept any restrictions that have to be placed on me— at least until I get involved in the Clarke program and even thereafter until I have restored through my actions and communications some level of trust that you feel comfortable with. Then we have a fighting chance. you are a very beautiful woman with a lot of fine points to your credit. You are a very caring mother as is evident by our two beautiful stable children.

Ten years ago I was at the end of my ropes and I asked God to find me a woman and he brought me you.

I don't want to throw that away and I hope you don't either. I want desperately to become normal in my thoughts and I beg you to put up with my inadequacies for the time being. We both look forward to a common future. I really do not want to lose the woman I love–The woman I love – You...Kellie

Please try and bear with me. I am open to compromise
Love Les xxxooo

Chapter Fifty-Two

Les was right. It was my ultimate goal to try to keep this family together. Les wasn't getting better and I started to doubt whether he ever would. But the events that followed demonstrated that something had to change.

It was the morning after enjoying a lovely trip to the mall. Sarah had taken ill with an extremely high fever and no matter what I did it didn't seem to want to break. I got the girls dressed and the four of us headed for the emergency room at the hospital. We were quickly shown to one of the vacant rooms. I noticed some blood on the floor that had been missed when the room had been cleaned and Sarah headed straight for it. I asked Les to hold the baby on the table for just a second so that I could pick Sarah up off the floor. I even placed his two hands on her tummy. "Just hold her," I repeated. As I went to pick up Sarah I turned my head only to watch our baby fall headfirst from the table onto the cement floor three feet below. I was so relieved when I heard her cries because it meant that she was alive!

The nurses came running quickly, followed by the doctor. Les just stood there, motionless, and said nothing. Again it was my family doctor who was on call that day. He did all the necessary checks and then sent Sophia with a nurse for a head scan. He wanted to ensure that her skull had not been crushed and that there was no internal bleeding.

When my doctor received the results of the test, Les was asked to go into the waiting room while my doctor took me into a separate room and shut the door. Dr. Frank was the most loving and compassionate man you would ever want to meet. But this day I saw a totally different side of him. He was angry and this filled me with fear. He spoke to me in a way I could not ignore. "Kellie, you are a great mom and you have been doing a wonderful job with these girls, but right now, as your doctor, I have to be straight with you. It is not safe to leave Les alone with your children, not for a minute, not even for a second. You were lucky this time. Nothing showed up on the test and Sophia is going to be okay, but from this moment on, Les is never to be left alone with your children. If he is, I will personally see to it that they are removed from your care."

Tears rolled down my face as he held my hand and said, "Please tell me you understand what I'm saying." I nodded to confirm that I understood and promised that I would not allow my husband to be alone with our children, not even for a second. At that moment I fully understood that the responsibility for the girls would be mine and mine alone. I would need to be on the alert twenty-four seven again.

Three days later I got my second letter.

Saturday Sept 13th 3:30 pm

Hello Sweetheart
Not feeling the greatest today. Don't know why but I do know I was feeling good the last few days and up days for me are usually followed by down days. At least that's the cycle I noticed and I'm sure you have as well.

I must say the past few days you have looked better than you ever have. Especially when you were dressed up like last night when you went out for a walk. You are a very elegant woman with an inner beauty that very few people are blessed with. And I thank my lucky stars that you stayed with me. I really enjoyed picking up those clothes for you and I hope to get the chance to see you in lots of other fabulous outfits. The world is a pretty mixed up place and we really only see the superficial side of people. I guess many people are haunted by their own personal demons and only a small fraction of people choose or get a chance to try and deal with them.

Well that's where I am right now— Right in the middle of dealing with a ton of issues that have been tied around my neck and have dragged me down for a long, long time. I am looking forward to talking to our doctor on Monday — I will tell him about what we talked about and the compromises I am willing to make. I will tell him about my mood swings as well. I really do not like them and I am sure you like them even less. I don't really notice them coming on and even when I am right in the middle of an aggressive phase I find it hard to see that I am really acting this way. I will try to make a conscious effort to avoid these swings or at least remove myself from the situation if one should occur again. I will tell my psychiatrist as well but I really do not wish to be on any more medication at least until I see the professionals at the Clarke. I think awareness plays a large part and that is where you can help me for the time being. I can enjoy my up days and be careful if I am having down days. Also I noticed you become stronger lately and that makes me feel good. I will say again that I don't think I've ever seen you look so beautiful as I have in the past week. It really makes me feel good and gives me a real desire to fight this, get stronger, get better, get healthy. And then we can get to know each other again. Please be patient with me–I LOVE YOU– Les

PS: This was a great idea and I love the opportunity to communicate. This way it allows me to share my feelings with you. Thanks, Les.

Chapter Fifty-Three

Our trip to the mall was the last time that Les ever got to be alone with our children. I became hypervigilant about everything that was going on around us. This was extremely stressful and took an even greater toll on my physical well-being. Memories of my childhood started flooding back and my body and mind remembered the stress of those days.

The little chat I had had with my doctor changed my whole outlook on how my life would play out. I now knew what to expect and I would have to learn how to cope alone. My focus and number one priority became my girls. I thought back to the times that I had been beaten, abused and neglected, and I wanted none of that for my girls. This triggered the fear that began to set in.

I felt paranoid knowing that all the responsibility was on me and that if something should go wrong I would be the one held accountable. I made sure I pulled up my socks and put on a brave face for the world and Les to see. I kept my feelings hidden even though I was really in a place of despair, fear and utter loneliness. Les was unaware of this, as were my girls. I endured in silence.

Chapter Fifty-Four

It seems so much of our life was now consumed with visiting doctor after doctor. As we were leaving for yet another appointment, Les handed me this next letter.

Monday Sept 15th 11:30 AM

Just finished relaxing with the Globe and trying to clear my head before I see the doctor. Hope you had a nice chat with Armanda.

I didn't sleep well at all again last night and I'm sure that contributes to the troubles of my mind. As a person needs proper rest in order to function properly and manage the stresses of everyday life. I guess for me the hardest part is the unknown. What exactly is wrong with me— How long will it last— Will it get better— Will it get worse—will it take a long time or will it take a short time. Or do I have a condition that I may have to live with forever. These all weigh heavily on my mind as I have you and the kids to think of. And when I am depressed I tend to dwell on it more. It may not be as bad as I imagine. It just seems to be taking a long time and I have myself to blame as I never had the courage to deal with the real problems I had earlier. But it's all out now and that's a relief. I just have the tension between my family to deal with and eventually get back on a more intimate level with you. If that is what the future holds for us, and I certainly hope it does. Les

After reading his letter I too realized how the lack of intimacy was affecting both of us. Holding, laughing and playing with our girls gave me warm fuzzies. I felt needed and loved and the girls gave me a reason to fight with all my might for my family. But I could not compare this to the feeling of intimacy I used to share with my husband. It had been almost two years since we had made love. Not that I didn't try, but I noticed that Les became even more stressed when he couldn't respond. His illness and the many medications he was taking continued to cause him to lose all desire. This meant our physical needs were not being met.

Taking care of the girls, making sure they were safe and making sure Les was safe around them, took all my strength. I had very little time for myself. This was not how I envisioned motherhood, nor did I think I would have ever found myself so far away from Les. He was the love of my life and he was changing before my eyes. I felt as if he had no control over this illness. What I could see was a man being stripped of all that he possessed.

The rest of the week passed and I saw very little of Les. I had noticed that he had been taking far too many sleeping aids, not enough to warrant a trip to the emergency room, but enough to cause me to be somewhat concerned. Eight days later a fourth letter was left in Sophia's crib along with a big broken heart drawn in red ink on the front. It read as follows.

Kellie JOYce

Sept 23,97 Tuesday

Hello Sweetheart,
Long time no write. Boy do I ever got a lot
of anxiety and nervousness that I'm trying
to contain. You mentioned today in
reference to Kim that you didn't have a lot
of patience. In reality, you have loads. You
don't realize it because of all the miracles
you are pulling off – Juggling so many
things. I thank God you are strong. Don't
kid yourself, you really are remarkable and
beautiful and youthful to boot.

I tell you I am on Pins and needles as I
wait to hear about my referral to the Clark
Institute and as the days go by I may get
more and more nervous. I think it is a
good Idea for me to go into the city
tomorrow – I would like to take the camera
and record a lot of the public sculpture
that is in the city. I will bring a note pad
so I can make notes about it as well. It will
really allow me to clear my head if even
it's just half a day. I want so much to
deal with my pain. I want so badly to have
a life.

I don't care if I am rich or poor, I just
want to be well. I know that I am a hard
working person with a kind heart. And if
you have that and peace of mind then
that's really all you need to start life
anew Till then, I will keep in control.
Love Les.

After writing this letter Les started to spiral downward and there seemed to be no end to his fall. I was getting really scared as his behaviours were becoming more bizarre and more out of control. The only person I could think of who could help me was Les' mother, so I picked up the telephone and called her in Newfoundland. She agreed to come up and spend a few weeks with us, using the grandchildren as an excuse for another visit. This way she hoped Les would not be suspicious. I didn't care. I just needed an extra pair of eyes.

Les' family really had no idea of how we were living. He had asked me to not give them details and for the most part I had respected my husband's wishes. But the reality of our life would soon be revealed.

Grace was great with the girls and I could see that they were good for her. But seeing her son so lost and alone was heartbreaking for her, as it would be for any mother. Les had often told me that his mom had her own daily struggles with depression. He had a huge respect for his mother and both of them seemed to understand how crippling mental illness could be. They both lived it. I believe they were better able to relate to each other. Their common interest in art and puzzles was an added blessing.

Chapter Fifty-Five

I had encouraged Les to enter a few pieces of his art in a local show being held in our community. It was no surprise that both of the pieces he submitted were accepted. I insisted he attend the Saturday opening of the show. It took a good bit of persuasion on my part, but he went.

The next morning I did not see him and I found another letter placed in the cupboard with my daily stash of chocolate. Les knew I would go there sometime during the day. His mom had taken Sarah out to the playground and Sophia was having her nap. I sat snuggled up with my tea and chocolate and I read his heartfelt words.

Sunday Sept 28

Feelings, nothing more than feeling whoa whoa whoa feelings. Feeling kinda strange as I know now that I do not have control. I was down to the glen art exhibition last evening, had a panic attack and had to leave shortly after I got there. Felt like I didn't belong and I felt that the people there could tell. It was a little bit scary!

Also yesterday at the mall I forgot how to walk. So I sort of shuffled my way along to a bench and then after a while the feeling passed and I knew how to walk again. Pretty scary stuff. I think I will take your earlier advice and buy some art supplies as I could use a creative outlet

138

and I have a lot of stocked finished and no shows to attend. So it's not like there is any pressure there. But I do feel the need for a creative outlet.

I may go to Wastewise and get some magazines to do some collages with. I have a lot of restless energy that I have to expel and I want to make sure that none of it comes out in the form of hostility.

Tomorrow I will take 2 pieces down and enter them into the Revision Juried Art Show I will also probably cut the lawns that will get rid of some energy. I hope we can get to take in a movie this week as it would be something I would look forward too.

Maybe we could have John and Gisela over for lunch someday as well. They are such nice company and don't forget about Rick and Sally.

Well I will see if mom and Sarah are around and I will come get you.

Don't forget we need salsa sauce.
love Les

Reading this I could see that his mind was racing. Les' thoughts and emotions were unpredictable and I didn't know what to expect from one moment to the next. Hours passed that day and there was no sign of him. The

Kellie JOYce

waiting game had begun again. His mom was worried sick so she made an appointment to see Les' doctor.

Early in the evening, just as the sun was going down, a very young police officer knocked at my door. He introduced himself then said, "Ma'am, your husband is going to be okay, but we have just admitted him to the hospital in Georgetown. The doctors have pumped his stomach and put him on suicide watch for the next forty-eight hours. Would you be able to bring him some personal belongings as his clothes are soiled?"

It had already been a stressful day. I had been dealing with so much. I'm sure the police officer saw this. "Can't it wait?" I snapped.

"May I come in?" he asked and I noticed sympathy in his voice.

"Sure," I moaned. I was exhausted, and on top of all that, I had a toothache that I had been ignoring for way too long. I felt as though I didn't want to have to deal with another attempt on his life again.

I said, "You know, one of these times when he cries out for help like this, he really will kill himself!" The police officer was very compassionate and stayed with me until Grace came back from the doctor's office. I explained why the officer was there and what had happened. I could see the relief on her face when she learned her son was going to be okay. I gathered together a few of Les' personal belongings. Grace agreed to stay with the girls while the police officer drove me to the hospital to visit my husband.

140

It was a somewhat silent ride as there was very little conversation. I cried and the officer respected the fact that I needed to release pent-up emotions. I hadn't wanted to break down in front of my kids or Grace, but in the police cruiser I felt safe to let it all go.

When I entered Les' hospital room he didn't say a word to me. He was still not responding to anyone. The nurse told me that he had been found under a bridge, smelling of booze and half naked. A few teenagers had spotted him and called the police.

It was in the middle of the day, for heaven's sake! I was feeling frustrated and at a loss as to what to do. I was told Les would be moved to Brampton as soon as a bed became available, hopefully within the hour. This time I didn't wait around. I felt useless and my own physical pain was escalating. Exhausted, I headed home.

The next morning the pain from my tooth forced me to go to the dentist and an emergency root canal was performed. I was sent home with strong painkillers and some antibiotics for the infection. I don't remember much of that evening as the medications totally knocked me out. I was fortunate that Les' mom was still with me as I was not sure there was anyone else upon whom I could rely. It is during times like this we reach out to family. I still had no contact with any of my family, but I was thankful to have Les' mom.

No one in the rest of Les' family wanted to talk about the possibility of his having a mental illness. Even though there was a strong genetic history of mental illness in the family, it was not discussed. Les' mom was the only member of his family who was not in denial. The rest of the family would not accept Les' diagnosis and instead looked for someone to blame. I was their target. At this stage of the game I had no energy left to deal with their ignorance. I maintained my focus on keeping my children and Les safe.

Chapter Fifty-Six

Just when you think it can't get any worse, it does. I answered a knock at the door and there, standing before me, was the police officer who had visited a few days before. You can imagine the panic that came over me. He saw it too and said, "This visit has nothing to do with your husband. I am here to see you."

I could sense my body starting to go numb. I had no idea why he would be here to see me. I invited him to come into the living room and Les' mom took the girls into the back yard. "Kellie, I am following up on a telephone report that was made to the station a few hours ago. A neighbor said they saw you outside the front of your house leaving your baby unattended and staggering as if you were drunk." I laughed with relief. I told the officer that I had had a root canal and had been taking drugs to combat pain and infection. I knew, of course, that the vindictive members of Les' family who lived in the neighbourhood were likely the source of the call, and I didn't mind saying so. I figured it was probably his cousin lashing out at me in his anger.

That telephone call prompted the Children's Aid to become involved and an enquiry was made as to my ability to be a fit mother. They wanted to see if I was able to raise the girls on my own since I would be alone due to my husband's illness. Follow-up meetings were scheduled as well as one with my family doctor. All of this just added more stress to my already stressful life.

Chapter Fifty-Seven

I visited Les a few times in the hospital and told him what had been happening at home. It seemed to weigh heavy on his mind, but since he was still my husband, he had a right to know what was happening. The third time I visited, he handed me a letter as I was leaving and said, "Just read it when you get a moment alone." I held him close and hugged him as if I never wanted to let go.

"Just get well," I whispered. "Just get well, Les."

When I got home I opened the letter. It was not dated.

Hi Sweetie,
Thanks for dropping by. Starting to come out of my down cycle. I figure by tomorrow I will be in what I consider to be a good frame of mind. I am not sure what was bringing me down. Did it have anything to do with mom being here? It is possible it depends on how much sleep I get and the more the merrier. HA!

Sometimes comments like Tammy made to you on the phone bring me down. Although I can't prevent people from speaking and I have to realize I will get a lot of judgemental responses to my condition. A lot of it being people's imaginations running wild as they don't know the whole story and try to create what they think is real to fill in the gaps. Also people seem to take some kind of sick pleasure out of other peoples' misery as if it makes them feel better or seem better than you. Or maybe this is just me rambling on. However I do know that I will have to develop a thick skin as I seek treatment as people can be pretty judgemental. And I think I have already told enough people more than enough. I hope this Children's Aid issue gets dealt with once and for all. I don't need this issue clouding things and you especially don't need it.

You can wear your nice outfit if you wish to impress them on Thursday, but after that I will wrap it up for Christmas.

It's nice to see the kids behaving so nicely and being on such good routines. It speaks very highly of your efforts as their mother. Thanks for bringing them in to see me. I know you hate them being in a place like this but it is where I am right now Thanks for your understanding and love. They are both so bright and mild mannered.

I hope you call the camera club and get involved in something you enjoy. Maybe we could clean out the space under the basement stairs and you could have your own darkroom there. :) Think about it, anything is possible.
Love Les

It was such a relief having his mom continue to stay with

me during this difficult time. I really did not enjoy taking the girls to see Les. After all, a psychiatric ward in a hospital was not the best place for Les to spend time together with his girls. But I knew how much their visits meant to him, so I took them, even though it was eating away inside of me. I tried hard to remain positive, but from what I could see, Les' condition was not being managed very well. It seemed no one really knew how to help him, sadly, not even I. Much of my stress was alleviated when Les was finally allowed to come home from the hospital.

I was grateful for a passion in photography. I took pictures of the girls daily and mounted them in photo albums. I had started to become more expressive and was actually getting pretty good. Les liked photography a lot as well, so perhaps that's why I enjoyed it so much. It was a part of me that I could share with him. My photos made him smile. Even though I felt helpless and was at a loss as to how to help him rekindle the spark that would light his fire, I thought perhaps photography was a way to help him want to live again. So I tried.

Chapter Fifty-Eight

It was the day I was to meet my doctor and a representative from Children's Aid. I knew I was a damn good mom, but I tell you, I was beginning to doubt myself. I remembered the times the Children's Aid Society had come to our house when I was a child. They had good reason to visit then, but not now. I kept telling myself that I was not like my mother. I was doing everything humanly possible to raise my girls and keep them safe. Yet it didn't seem to matter! The fact that someone in authority would even question my ability caused my body to tremble with fear.

That morning I had awakened to find a beautiful bouquet of flowers and another letter. Even in Les' darkest moments he knew me; he could read me. He had been up before me, following his morning routine of going to McDonalds and reading the newspaper while drinking a coffee. It was usually during these times that he would write to me.

Hi Sweetie,
This paper placemat was the only thing I had to write on today. I knew they would have them at their counter. I never got much sleep last night so I am a bit on edge today. Maybe later in the afternoon we can take our walk together after your appointment. You are doing nice work on the photo album and perhaps you should take it with you when you go see that Bitch from Children's Aid today.

147

Kellie JOYce

*I hope these flowers lift your spirits. My
heart is in the right place it is my mind
that is screwed. I know I've become more
and more distant and turned inwards
towards myself but the fact of the matter is
I am at a critical junction in my life. I'm
trying so hard to contain myself, and that
is taking all my energy. I just want to be
given the chance to go to the Clarke and
trust in their professional judgement and
follow whatever path they show me to get
well mentally. I know how terribly painful
this must be for you and how awfully alone
you must feel. I am constantly aware of
that and just how fragile the state of our
lives are right now. I just want to be given
the chance to turn it around because you
would have to be crazy to want to be living
the way I am living right now. AND not to
mention taking you and the girls along for
the ride! Well I don't think I'm crazy
because I want the help of the professionals
to cure myself.*

*I think I will call the Doctor today and ask
about my referral. I will also cancel my
appointment with the acupuncturist. You
should call the camera club and get some
information about their group. :)*

*Please accept these flowers and know that
the real me that's buried behind the pain
loves you very much. Your one of a kind.
Love Les*

Les knew this was what I needed that day. Even through all his pain my husband was able to comfort me and make me feel strong.

When I got to the doctor's office I was ushered in right away. The lady from Children's Aid started asking my doctor all kinds of personal questions. He abruptly cut her off. "That is irrelevant and not why you are here, so why don't we address the real issues? You want to know if Kellie is a good mother, so listen carefully to what I have to say."

What he said next absolutely blew me away. "I have a lot of women who come into this office and I could understand if you were questioning me about one or two of them. But this woman standing before you is one of the best mothers I have ever known. She does not neglect her children's needs. The girls' medical care and their shots are up to date. I believe we are done." I was pleasantly surprised at his faith in me.

"You can ask me or my doctor anything you want to know. I have nothing to hide," I told the lady. She looked at me and said, "There is no need for that," and, thanking my doctor for his time, she left.

After she had gone I had a moment alone with my doctor. He looked at me with such compassion, understanding and approval. "You are a strong, unique and wonderful woman and mother, and no one deserves to make you feel otherwise." I wanted to hug him at that moment, but I knew that would not be the orthodox thing to do. I couldn't help thinking back to the way I felt that time in the courtroom when the judge had spoken directly to me.

My doctor had just made me feel very much the same way. It was as if I been found innocent of a crime I didn't commit. I felt proud. Neglecting the needs of my children, not putting them first, I never wanted to be found guilty of that! Later I sent my doctor a thank you card letting him know just what his words that day meant to me.

Les wrote me another letter that day. I found it on my pillow.

Hi Sweetheart,
I am proud of the way you handled Children's Aid today. Very professional and you were dressed to kill. Sure put her in her place. Wouldn't be hard to fly with you in Executive class with you dressed like that.

Your chutney is really delicious. You have a natural ability in the kitchen and that can really help you prosper down the road.

Taking the kids to the drop off centre sounds like a good idea too. We may meet some really nice people out of it.

I am struggling with my emotions still and been keeping everything bottled up too long and suppressed everything to my detriment and everyone else's.

I hope when I see my doctor on Monday that they may have some news for me. It would be nice to have a date in mind that I can work towards. It would ease my mind somewhat!

I would really like to effectively become a normal human being for once and for all. I know it will be hard making the transition but I know that I can maintain control of my faculties until then. Especially now that we have a compromise in place.

Don't be afraid to tell me anything that's on your mind as sometimes not knowing is worse as your mind wanders and thinks of bad things. I guess that's only human nature. I hope you realize that through these letters which are sometimes a struggle, that it is a healthy way for me to express what I am feeling.

I have so many positive ideas that just need to get my mental health in order to allow these ideas to come to fruition. I want to help and support you in every way I know how I will always be here for you and I know that you are there for me. I respect the fact that you realize that we have two helpless infants needs that must be met first at all cost. You are a very strong person and I am so happy that I asked God to find me a woman and he found you.
Love Les :)

Chapter Fifty-Nine

Les didn't write to me as often any more and he had stopped dating his letters. Actually I hadn't received any for quite some time. I would remind him that I really appreciated his letters and that they were a source of great support for me. But it didn't help. I knew that, as much as he wanted to stay in control and help me understand his daily struggles, he couldn't. At times I felt he was unaware of the passing of days as, for him, one day just rolled right into the next. He walked around in a daze, exhibiting a sadness and pain that only grew. In between the long gaps of silence I was losing more and more of my husband to his illness and his fight to overcome it. Our girls started to fear being around him. This was hard for me to watch. They were so young, just babies, and yet they could sense his anxiety and fear it. Sarah clung to my leg or wanted to be in my arms almost every waking minute.

I was fortunate that both of the girls were good sleepers and would sleep through the night. At this stage Les was awake at all hours and slept very little, except when he took his medications. He would often take medication that was not regulated or monitored by me. If I tried to intervene, his anger would grow, so I didn't interfere. He said he wanted to be in control of the medications he took as it gave him a little bit of dignity. I knew from reading his previous letters that he was feeling out of control, yet he wanted to be able to say he had some control remaining.

Despite what I saw, I also knew it was better to respect him as a person and allow him to make his own choices.

"Don't treat me like a baby, Kel. I'm your husband," he would say. "I know what I'm doing. Why does everyone treat me like a kid, like I'm fucking crazy? Just stop, okay!"

The man I had married would never have spoken to me like that. But the man I had married was gone, and no matter how hard I tried, I could not bring him back.

Chapter Sixty

Thanksgiving arrived and I was pleasantly surprised when Les returned from McDonalds with a coffee in one hand and a letter in the other. "Kel, I've got to go into the city today. I need to be away from you and the girls. I'm okay. I just need to be alone." And off he went. I didn't question his choice. I was thinking that I needed the break as well.

I held his letter in my hand and debated whether or not I had the strength to read it today. By now I was feeling overwhelmed and even more helpless. All I could think was 'What if? What if this was another suicide note?' I decided I had better read it. I took the baby monitor and my coffee out into the back yard, sat on the grass and read my husband's mind. These letters were just that, an insight into his mind. They were all I had to help me understand what he was thinking, as he never spoke to me otherwise. What he had written today came as a pleasant surprise and provided me with a flicker of hope.

Hello Honey,
This Thanksgiving I wish to give thanks to you. For having you here in my life to keep my spirits up and give me something to live for, both you and our two gorgeous children. I know it must trouble you when you see me staring off into space, or when my mind wanders from simple things I should be able to concentrate on. It has been a long time and I am sure it has taken a toll on you as well as me. I find I am mostly disturbed at not knowing myself

for all these years and falling pray and giving in to the dark side of my thoughts. I wish I had the strength to fight this years ago, but I just seemed to want to always punish and self doubt myself. So I would give into temptation and pay the price with horrible guilt. Guilt that kept me from ever being truly at ease with myself for so long that I don't know what being at ease really means anymore. Sometimes I really loosen up and act kinda crazy like the night we were playing cards. Nights like that I really feel at ease but I know I will pay for it later with guilt and depression. I Know I don't deserve to keep beating myself up and blaming myself for the past. It is just a self repeating cycle to keep knocking myself down to the point where I had nothing about myself to feel good about. And that is sort of like part of my illness as it is so much like moms way of beating herself up. Having all this time off and no real medical help, at least progressive help has been frustrating. I hope the Lithium works on my mood as the mood swings are really unbearable both on me and you and the family. It will be nice to get away for part of the day and go somewhere I enjoy. I should try and put that in my daily routine. I want to buy a book and the kids can keep it for me till Christmas. Thanks for being there and keeping the family together. You are the Rock which I look to for stability.
Love Les

Chapter Sixty-One

Our babies encountered a lot of their first milestones. You know the ones: first crawl, first steps, first teeth, first words. These were the exciting moments that, as parents, you look forward to sharing with each other. But I had no one with whom I could share. At least that's how I felt. Most of the time I didn't really have time to enjoy these moments either. It was only on the days that Les would take time for himself and go out, that I got some alone time with the girls. To be able to enjoy them in all their beauty without having to be on constant alert was a very special time for me. The daily vigilance was really taking a toll on my body, but I knew I had to ignore my pain and the symptoms and remain strong. The girls needed me.

I continued to have a lot of conversations with myself, but only internally. My mind seemed to be racing all the time, never slowing down, never taking a break. It was like being in a room with twenty people all talking at the same time. That's how fast my mind was running.

Les had been off work for a year and a half now. We were being taxed financially and the burden was becoming harder to bear. Before Les became ill he had made all the financial decisions. Now I was forced to make them myself. I knew we had some RRSP's that we had saved for a rainy day. Since it was pouring rain outside, today seemed like a good time to discuss our options. I sat Les down so we could talk. It amazed me how clearly he was able to think in some moments and then in others, nothing. He did agree, however, that it would be beneficial if we paid off our debts. Now it was only our mortgage that we would have to manage. Realizing I would have to take control of this hit me hard. The harsh reality of his illness was sinking in. The Les I had known, who could manage and control financial situations like no other, was no longer able to pay even a few bills on time, let alone budget our money. The thought of that really scared me! I didn't show it, but I was definitely alarmed.

Chapter Sixty-Two

After we made the decision to pay off our bills, Les appeared to be more upbeat and I even got to hear him laugh a bit. It seemed to me that the more daily routines he had in place, the better he responded in situations. He liked routine and it became a way for me to help him. We began taking daily walks in the evenings. The morning routines were already established. For a while Les even started to do artwork every day. He wasn't able to paint with a one-haired paintbrush like he used to do, so instead he decided to do miniature paper collages. He would sit and cut pictures from the magazines he picked up at Wastewise and separate these into sections. One of the pieces he created was a stunning picture of leaves falling from a tree. It was made solely from women's lips, arms and legs. It was fascinating to see how he had pieced together different sizes of lips to make the leaves on the tree while the branches were made from the women's arms and legs.

I loved to watch him work. He was not only a perfectionist in all he did, but he was also a man of passion. When he worked I got to see that side of Les again. I was able to see that look in his eye, that same look he once had for me. I too am a passionate person and I felt that much of the pain I was experiencing then was due to the fact that I couldn't physically express this, just like I couldn't express my fears and my anger, in fact, any of the emotions I felt. I had to bury them all inside. What a hole I was digging, but I did the things I had to do in order to maintain my strength.

Chapter Sixty-Three

Les decided that we should go out and treat ourselves by shopping at the mall. We didn't really have the extra money to be doing this but we needed to boost our morale. Shopping sometimes has a way of doing that. Les bought a few more canvasses and we got the girls Santa Claus outfits to wear when it came time to have their Christmas pictures taken. And, of course, I got myself clothes. A new outfit was the one feel-good treat that seemed to bring me to my happy place. Perhaps that had something to do with my childhood as we rarely, if ever, got new clothes.

I knew I was overcompensating by buying new clothes for myself and by providing the girls with the best of everything. Although I was consciously aware of this, I did it anyway. I didn't try to hide that from anyone. It was far too obvious that this was what was happening.

After we got home from the mall, for the first time in weeks, Les wrote me another letter.

Hi Sweetheart,
Had a fun afternoon with you. I love when you buy flattering clothes. It's great to see the expression on your face when you find something that really suits your mood and personality. You can be a lot of fun to be with and I love being a part of that fun, because it makes me feel good. I may have acted a bit off but I was feeling pretty good this afternoon. However I know that I have a lot of unresolved emotional pain to

deal with. It's nearly five o'clock and I just remembered that it's too late to call the doctor. Maybe tomorrow.

Thanks for making such an important decision to pay off our loans and get that monkey off our backs. I admire your strength. I struggle everyday with my feelings and I try hard to stay stable enough to be sociable and take part in child rearing, but I have a tremendous amount of what I would call "bother" on my mind. I really can't wait to spill my guts to the Clarke Institute so that I can start over. I know nothing will happen overnight but I have always believed in happy endings. That is what kept me going all these years.
love Les
xxxooo

Chapter Sixty-Four

I needed to do something for myself to forget about my problems at home. The wait time to get help for Les had been so long and the lack of support and information to help me understand Bipolar Disorder was almost non-existent. This caused enormous frustration and I just couldn't be alone in my thoughts anymore. I had to show my face, to be visible and speak out about this. I wanted to be heard and I wanted answers. I had already asked my doctor if there were any support groups in our community that could help me deal with Les' illness, but he had said there weren't any. So I joined the local Toastmasters group instead. This was a public speaking group and I was so looking forward to openly expressing my concerns. I felt that going to Toastmasters would offer me a challenge and allow my voice to be heard.

I stood up in front of the club members to deliver my first speech. It was the introductory speech, the one you give to let the group know who you are. I stood up there in front of everyone, with no cue cards, and spoke like a pro. That night I won an award for being the top speaker and I won every other time thereafter, except for my last speech, which was, as I now see it, nothing more than a cry for help.

When my husband wanted to be heard he would take a bottle full of pills with alcohol. I chose to write, one powerful speech after another. But this last night my speech didn't go very well, and I broke down in a stream of tears, opening my soul to the thirty odd people in the room. I believe that every one of them who listened was crying also. It was not the best speech I had delivered;

161

however, it was poignant enough to touch them just the same. The positive feedback I received was overwhelming, and, even though I wasn't the top speaker, I saw the importance of being real. I had stopped wearing a mask and had allowed others to see and feel my pain. I knew then how powerful and influential words could be, and I knew one day that I would have to come back to this place. I also knew I couldn't deal with it now.

That last speech I gave at Toastmasters was about bringing awareness to others regarding mental health. Keeping silent about the issues involved wasn't working and I knew I needed to be heard. I wanted to start that conversation, to start people talking. Some of the written messages I received from my peers that evening read "Kellie, fight for change." "You speak with such passion." "You need to be heard and change needs to happen." "It was hard to listen to your speech." "Having a mother who has suffered from depression all her life, I respect and honour your courage." "WOW! I have never heard such a provocative speech. Never give up."

I couldn't continue going to Toastmasters as my home life was crumbling. So I stayed home, smiling, taking care of the kids, and supporting my husband in the only ways I knew. I continued wearing a mask. But I never gave up. The writing continued in my head.

Show Your Face

We don't always admit it
But we are split
All live in the same world
Yet are worlds apart
Where to start
Unravel the web we weave
It is self-evident, diverse
Our shadow side, a curse
Fighting to survive
Learning to live
Learning to love
One another
And ourselves
Two faces
Looking but not seeing
Divided
Show Your Face

Kellie JOYce – August 2012

Chapter Sixty-Five

Because of Les' downward spiral, it was hard for me to take time for myself. Until now there had been no pressure for Les to return to work, but the company notified him that his two years would soon be up and he would then be taken off long-term disability. We were still awaiting a call for his assessment at the Clarke Institute where we hoped he could possibly get some real help.

The letters were written less frequently and Les often repeated the same things, yet I felt grateful every time I received one. I got this letter out of the blue after I had asked him if he was worried about going to the Institute. Somehow Les had found the strength to write down his thoughts. These words provided me with a glimpse into his reality.

Hi Sweetie,

I'm not worried I'm just preoccupied with my thoughts. It is quite possible that I have an illness in addition to whatever trauma I've experienced. But I am willing to put my faith in the professionals. I must admit that it does shake me up somewhat. Mostly the fear of the unknown. What do I have?

How do I get better? Is it really Bipolar Disorder? How will it affect you and the kids? How long will it take? I do know deep down that I am a good hardworking individual who would love to have fun if I can get the help I need. I am glad I am not getting hassles from Air Canada so far as I don't really have any day to day stability and I am quite shaken up most of the time. That's why I like to get out everyday and read the Globe, it takes my mind off everything and I don't have to think about anything or pretend to be anyone. I have an incredible amount of anxiety today. Very overpowering! I am doing my best to keep it in check. Thanks for breakfast and for the coffee.

Love
Les

Chapter Sixty-Six

Christmas was only a couple of weeks away and I really found this time of the year difficult. Family gatherings, sharing good food and buying that special someone in your life the perfect gift that would bring a smile were the things I missed the most. Les and I had always made Christmas a big deal before we had kids. Now that we had children of our own, it was all about them. It made the holidays somewhat easier knowing that I could focus on my kids, yet it seemed that, at Christmas time, my thoughts were of my mom and how I wished she were in my life. Fifteen years had passed and I still felt that void.

Les and I decided to take the kids home to Newfoundland for the holidays. Because he had worked for Air Canada, we had passes to travel, and once there, we could stay with his parents. I think Les knew how much I was longing to see my mother. She had never met her grandchildren and maybe this time she would get the opportunity.

I was right. We were visiting with one of my aunts and, while my father was napping, my mom had sneaked out of the house for a quick visit with her grandchildren. This was the first time I had seen my mother in years. I was filled with mixed emotions and was really uncertain as to how to respond. I didn't have to worry however, as the meeting was very brief. My mom remarked that Sarah looked just like me when I was a baby. I actually saw her smile when she looked into Sarah's eyes and again when she held Sophia up in the air over her shoulders trying to make her laugh. I felt a fleeting moment of bliss, and then it was gone. During the short time my mom stayed, I was able to take a few pictures of her with my girls. I knew this would probably be the only time she ever got to see or hold the girls. Again I was right. So it was back to the reality of no mom for me, no grandmother for my girls.

When I got home to Les' parents after the visit, I pretended that nothing unusual had happened. "Did you have a nice visit with your family, honey?" Les asked. A simple "Yes" was all I replied. I could see my husband was in pain and I wanted to put on a brave face for him, not add to his pain. The brave face was a tool I had learned for survival. I had obviously used my mask many times before and I had become quite good at it. It was better than dealing with reality.

I was glad I hid my pain because later that evening, after the girls were in bed, Les lay next to me and handed me another letter. "Can we just hug Kel, before you read it?" he asked. "I need to be held." Les fell asleep next to me that evening. We had not lain like this in over two years. This was where we had met, where Les and I had first hugged lying down together some ten years earlier. This brought me back to that moment in time. As we lay there with our bodies entwined I once again felt as if we were one. No one had ever made me feel like that.

I fell asleep and awoke in the same spot and in the same embrace. We had not moved and our bodies seemed to have meshed together. We used to call it our 'magical skin'. I was still holding the letter Les had given me and I was anxious now to see what my husband had written. It was strange that Les was still asleep. I guess he had taken a couple of extra sleeping pills because it was midday before he got up. I had already given the girls a bath and fed them before I took the time to read his letter.

Hi Sweetheart,
Pretty depressed today but don't know why.
Just wish it wouldn't happen. It is even
hard to write about it but I know I must
try. It is a vicious cycle being up some
days and down the next. When you are up
and feeling good you think you've got this
thing beat and then you wake up feeling
terrible for no reason at all, it's quiet
strange. I say for no reason at all but I
am sure there is a medical reason for it.
I'm just glad I realize it is happening
and don't get frustrated and take it out on
you and the kids which is really unfair.
When I get like this I find it hard to see
the light at the end of the tunnel and I am
unsure as to how long it will last. I know I
really don't have anything to despair about
but I can't prevent my mind from slipping
into this state. It really pisses me off!!!!
This has taken me a long while to write as
it so hard to put my thoughts down on
paper. I hope you understand that I know
this is temporary. I am just right now
smack dab in the middle of everything.
Thanks for your support,
Les

We had planned to stay in Newfoundland for a longer time but Les felt that being around his parents in their home was causing him to fall into a deeper depression. I too was feeling uncomfortable and finding it hard to fit in where we didn't belong. That's what it felt like we were trying to do. We did stay for Christmas dinner and then later that evening we took a flight back to Toronto.

For Sophia the plane ride home was brutal as she was suffering from a cold and she was so stuffed up. She shrieked all the way home, while Sarah and Les sat in the seat across from us. Her crying didn't stop until the plane landed. I felt so drained. When at last we opened the front door of our townhouse, I let out a huge sigh of relief. Before putting Sophia to bed I gave her an extra spoonful of Tylenol to help ease her pain so that she and I could get a good night's sleep. It worked!

Kellie JOYce

Mother

I went to your funeral today
Yet, you are still alive
I said my good-bye's and
Sat at peace with myself
And our relationship

I have longed for your tenderness
Wished for your respect and love
Needed your guidance
So I thought

Now I find myself
At a turning point in my life
Without the
Longing
Waiting
Hoping

Accepting our relationship
For what it is
Or isn't

Accepting you
For who you are
Or aren't

I'm allowing myself to enjoy a life
With my mother by my side
Realizing I have had many mothers
Along the way
You included

I'm grateful for that
I accept that
And I thank you Mom
For doing all that you could

I say good-bye as
I feel joy, peace and
Sadness in my heart
And that's okay.

Kellie JOYce – June 2006

Chapter Sixty-Seven

Les went out for his early morning coffee and the newspaper and returned with a brown paper bag on which he had scribbled a few words. The words were barely visible and I had a hard time trying to decipher what he had written.

Hi Sweetheart,

I know how you feel at holiday times now. It has really hit me hard. The sense of aloneness, isolation and despair. I still hope we can find it within ourselves to celebrate Christmas together even if it is just the four of us. Maybe we could visit John and Gisela. I feel like I've, or should I say, we've been robbed of so much that we shouldn't let them steal our dignity. We may not be exactly happy but we can do the best we can under the circumstances.

I feel really lost right now, like a sailboat that is spinning in circles in the middle of the ocean.

It seems to be so far from my dreams that I don't know that I will ever get to them. I have very little self confidence or self will to accomplish anything. It is very hard to shake this off. I think I will do something write now about it and go clean the van

We managed to get through the rest of the holiday season without any trips to the hospital. Les and I spent a very quiet New Year's Eve. He had insisted we stay at home as he didn't want to be around people. We didn't have big goals and plans any more. We just wanted to take things day by day.

Chapter Sixty-Eight

On January 10, 1999 we finally got the call for which we had been waiting. Les was scheduled to meet with the professionals at the Clarke Institute. We had been waiting for that telephone call for a year and a half, since the day he had been referred. I was so fed up with our medical system!

Les' illness and pain were not caused by a broken arm or leg. He had no visible cuts or bruises, so the fact that he needed help was not obvious. I felt that he had been neglected and put on hold for far too long. The wait had killed his spirit and filled his mind with negative thoughts. He desperately wanted a way out. Earlier in the day he had openly admitted that he wanted to die and I had begged and pleaded with him to have the faith and strength to want to get better for the sake of his girls. I wanted him to keep fighting until he had an appointment at the Clarke Institute. I wanted him to wait and see what they had to say.

"You've waited this long, Les. Just hang in there a little while longer. I have faith that they will help you. Please, please go and get the help you need and come back healthy for your girls and me." Les cried like a baby but he didn't want me to console him.

"I need to go and write, Kel. Maybe I can try to write what I'm feeling." He later presented what would be the last letter he ever wrote to me.

Hello Sweetheart
A day of mood swings so far. Fast as

lightening. I am very troubled by last nights news. Even more so that I am not getting any sleep and compounded by the fact that I am now on lithium. All which doesn't make me feel too good. I was in a good mood despite the lack of sleep when I woke up. Cleaned up the kitchen and cleaned with the vacuum and felt great of the job I had done. The place was looking great with the two of us working well together. Then I just got really mad, hostile, angry for no reason. I can't explain it I was up a lot of the night last night worrying about my upcoming visit to the Clarke. Since I have been off of loxapil I have had trouble sleeping again. I am very worried about having to talk about all the things I am terribly ashamed of and have to relive a lot of painful memories. Maybe thinking about that makes my mood swings so quickly, or maybe, it's an inherited Mental disorder. I guess time will tell. Kel , you know I am not a spiteful person, but sometimes I would like to kill all the fucking bastards that get in our way and cause us problems. It gets hard to stay on an even keel and I really pray that the Clarke Institute will be of help to me. If they can't help, I don't know what to do or where to turn. I just hope you can bear with me in the meantime.
Love Les

Chapter Sixty-Nine

The day for the visit to the Clarke Institute arrived. The long wait to be assessed in order to get the help Les needed was finally over. He was a basket case. His whole body trembled due to his extremely high anxiety level. We both had so much riding on this assessment, but it didn't go as we had expected.

The day after Les was admitted I once again got a home visit from a tall, skinny blonde-haired man who worked for Children's Aid. This was the first time I had ever encountered a male representative. Not that it mattered, but I was surprised. He looked not more than twenty-one. I could tell that he had not made many home visits so I invited him to come inside and have tea and some scones. I guess I was trying to make him feel at ease.

My girlfriend, Tammy, was visiting that day and I could tell that her presence made him feel uncomfortable. I reassured him by saying that anything he had to discuss with me was okay to say in front of Tammy. He blushed and didn't really know what to say.

"I'm confused. Why are you here?" I asked. "I thought my case was closed after my doctor spoke to the other worker."

"I know nothing about that," he said. "I am here to talk about your husband."

"My husband? He is in the hospital. Why would you be here because of him?"

"Ma'am, are you sure you don't want to have this conversation privately?" he asked, his voice quivering. Hearing that, Tammy dressed our children and took them out into the back yard.

"You are really freaking me out now," I told the worker. "What is going on with my husband?"

I was not prepared for what he said next. He spoke gently, saying, "He has finished his initial assessment at the Institute and we have been notified of the results."

"So soon?" I asked.

"Ma'am?"

"Would you please stop calling me ma'am? My name is Kellie."

He nodded his head and continued. "Kellie, based on the information that your husband provided to the doctors at the Clarke Institute, we are here to inform you that he will not be allowed to return home."

"Are you crazy? Of course he can come home. No one is going to stop him from coming home." My anxiety was becoming obvious.

"I'm having a hard time saying this, Kellie. As you have probably guessed, I am new at this. What I am trying to say is that Les' doctor contacted us to let us know that Les is a threat to you and your girls. Based on this new information he will not be allowed to return to the family home. You will have to find him a place to live before we

177

release him. If you don't abide by these conditions, I will have to remove your kids and put them in our care."

"You're crazy! My girls aren't going anywhere! And you're telling me that my husband can't be with us? For how long?"

"I don't know all the details."

I stopped him before he had a chance to say anything further. "What do you mean, you don't know all the details?"

I got up from my seat and started pacing the floor. "This can't be happening. Where is he going to go?"

"I have a statement for you to sign acknowledging that you understand what will happen if your husband returns home."

I signed the paper, fully understanding what he had just said to me. But I didn't want to believe it.

Chapter Seventy

I remained in shock long after the Children's Aid worker left our home. Tammy tried to get me to see the positive side of things after I had told her what the worker had said. "Look at it this way, Kel. They made the decision for you. No one can blame you for that decision. And you know their job is to protect children. They have made this decision to protect your girls and, for that reason alone, you must be grateful."

I was now forced to tell Les' family what was going on. For so long I had been protecting him, fighting this battle, mainly on my own and in silence. So many thoughts were storming through my mind. Was Les again thinking of killing us all? That was my initial thought. And then it hit me. Les must be devastated if he has been told that he can't come home to his family. He had put his faith in the assessment and had waited all this time only to be told that he couldn't come home. I had to go and see him, but not before finding him a place to stay. Coming home was no longer an option.

That was easier than I expected. Les' aunt and uncle lived in town and they agreed to go and see him. They said they would discuss with him the possibility of his staying with them for a while until he found another place. Once that was taken care of, I was off to see Les only to learn that he had been moved to the mental illness facility in Oakville. It seemed he had once again threatened to kill himself. I asked a friend of mine to drive me to Oakville so I could see him.

"What reason do I have to live, Kel?" Les spoke as if there

were no life left in him at all.

"I've found you a place to stay, Les," I told him.

"I know, Kel," he said. "My aunt and uncle were here. They told me I could stay with them as long as I didn't talk to HER. HER has a name I told them, and it's Kellie. She's my wife and I don't want you to ever fucking say another bad word about her."

Les continued, "I would have slit my aunt's throat if she fucking said another bad word about you. I think I scared her to death." Les started to laugh. I laughed with him. We laughed together in our pain.

"Because I punched the mirror thinking it was glass during that visit from my aunt and uncle, everything in this room has been removed. I will be here for quite a while, Kel," he went on to say. I thought that this was the best option anyway as I could only visualize this scenario playing out one way.

"I got another referral," Les said with disgust. "It is for Stonewood Health Centre. Wonder how long I'll have to wait this time."

Chapter Seventy-One

The next six months were the most unsettling times I went through with Les. We had to get a separation agreement so that he would be able to visit his girls. In the agreement the judge spelled out his rights. He was able to visit any time he wished as long as it was acceptable with me. Another adult or myself had to be present during these visits.

Although Les wasn't allowed to live in our home, he had been allowed supervised visits so I encouraged him to visit daily. I hoped that these visits would be the incentive that would make him feel life was worth living.

Les' visits, however, were sporadic. He would visit one day and not show up the next. Between visits I learned of yet other suicide attempts. Within six months he had made three attempts to end his life. At least they were the three I knew about.

Les was making all kinds of weird decisions, like deciding to live in his van that summer. I helped by letting him shower at the house and by cooking extra meals for him. In spite of all his pain, he would still praise me and tell me what a great cook I was.

Les gave away most of his personal belongings. What little he had left he asked if he could store at my place. Each time I saw Les I would see a new transformation. Some days I would see a man already dead, a man who had no emotion, no sense of direction and no real purpose for living. He would sometimes appear to be lost or broken like shattered glass. Other days I would glimpse brief moments where I felt I was looking into the eyes of the man I had married. But those moments were too brief.

"Kel, no matter what I tell you or how good I look and feel, don't ever trust me to be alone with the girls, okay?" he said to me one day. I could easily promise him that because Children's Aid had already made that decision for us. But for him to say that out loud to me must have taken great strength and self-awareness.

I had known for a long time that it was not safe for Les to be alone with the girls. I wanted him to be able to see his girls, but I wasn't taking any chances. I wanted to make sure they were safe. I had confided all of this to a friend and neighbour. She too was a stay-at-home mom, like me. If she saw Les' van in the driveway, she would stay out on her front lawn until he left. It was as if I had an extra pair of eyes, watching and protecting us. Sometimes, if I thought she was not aware that Les was visiting, I would use the excuse that I needed a cup of sugar or something and call her. Then she would pop over.

The MS symptoms compounded my worries. My body continued to grow weaker. I tried to hide this from Les and continue to wear a mask.

Chapter Seventy-Two

On one of Les' visits, seeing that he was in the mood to talk, I felt it was a good time to share my concerns with him. I could speak frankly with him and that was how he preferred it. "One of these days you are actually going to succeed, Les," I told him. "You can't keep doing this to your body, and I don't feel it is a good idea to keep allowing our girls to see you this way. I worry that you are going to end up killing yourself. Is that what you want?"

There was a long pause, then, "I'm gonna fight this, Kel, just wait and see. Maybe Stonewood can help me. I have an appointment next week."

That was late summer and Les spent only two weeks in Stonewood. He said he couldn't stand listening to everyone's stories. He said no one would listen to him. He wanted to deal with the dreams he was having, as they were so vivid and disturbing. "We don't deal with dreams in here," he had been told. He told me he had lied to get out of Stonewood and that it had been easy. It was what he didn't tell me that soon became obvious.

Chapter Seventy-Three

Shortly after, Les left Stonewood. It was a beautiful crisp evening in the late fall. This was Les' favourite time of the year. He had come to the house to visit the girls and me. He was so happy this day. He had found a new apartment and had come to remove a lot of his stuff from my place. He asked me to keep all of his art stored at my house because he wanted his girls to have it. I didn't argue with him as I had plenty of room in my basement. Les played with the girls and he laughed a lot. We shared a tasty grilled salmon lunch together and spent a few hours out in the front yard doing some gardening. It was wonderful to see him in such good spirits.

"May I hold Sophia for just a moment?" he asked. I was standing about a foot away so I agreed. I watched how he picked her up, so lovingly, so gracefully. His smile for her was genuine. When he put her down, he thanked me for giving him that moment with her. He told me how much he appreciated my letting him hold Sophia.

I remember that he left that afternoon and then he came back into the house to ask if there was anything he could get for me. "No thanks, Les," I replied.

"You sure?" he said in the funny voice he used to use. At that moment I saw the old Les again. He had given me yet another glimmer of hope.

I was feeling rather pleased about the day's events so I put the girls in the stroller and headed uptown for a late evening treat. As I thought back to Les' mood, I got a sick feeling in the pit of my stomach. I realized he was on another one of his highs again, thinking everything was wonderful and that he could fight his nemesis. I knew this mood was always followed by a low.

When I returned home after our walk that evening, I found Les had left a beautiful message on the answering machine. He wished the girls 'sweet dreams' and told them what a fun day Daddy had had. I tried to call him back so he could speak to them, but there was no answer. That sick feeling in my stomach grew, and grew...

Chapter Seventy-Four

Les made us all forget he was sick that beautiful fall day. The next morning around nine o'clock I answered a knock at the door. It was his brother's wife's friend. "Hi, Kellie. I'm Janette. Do you remember me? We met once at Derek's and Joan's home."

"Not really," I said, "but do come in. My friend and I have a house full of kids this morning because it's a PA day at school. On days like today we help each other out." Sophia was clinging to my leg.

"I need to talk to you alone, Kellie," she said in a faint voice. "It's important. Can we step out onto the porch and talk?"

Now I didn't know this lady, but there she was, at my door, telling me she had something important to talk about. I said, "Okay. Would you like a cup of coffee? Come in. It's warmer inside."

She insisted we talk on the front porch. "Kellie, I'm here about Les."

"Les? Why are you here about Les?"

"He killed himself last night."

"NO! NO! You're a fucking liar. He did not! Why are you telling me this? Why are you here? Why isn't a police officer telling me this? No! No! NO! NO! Go away. Get off my property. I don't even know you!"

I was in a state of rage. Even though I had had a sick feeling in my stomach the previous day, I didn't want to believe her. Then I started to scream. The neighbours could hear my screams and came running over to see what was going on. "Just get that fucking liar off of my property," I kept yelling.

It took a while for me to calm down, and when the news did sink in, Janette wanted to give me more details. She didn't need to tell me. "He jumped off a bridge, didn't he?" I asked her.

"How do you know that?" she replied.

"He once told me that if the day came and he really wanted to die, he would jump off a bridge just to make sure he succeeded."

By now I could barely walk or talk. My screams had turned to tears and then I was crying uncontrollably. "How am I going to tell his girls? How am I going to tell them their daddy is gone?"

I sat in fetal position on my front porch and stayed there until the police arrived. They informed me that Derek had been called to the scene. Apparently Les had left a suicide note asking him to take care of any loose ends. The police officer said that Les had jumped off the bridge at Highway 410 onto the shoulder of the Highway 401. He said he had chosen a smart way to die because no one else had been involved or hurt.

"He left three notes and one was addressed to your daughters," the officer said as he handed the note to me.

Kellie JOYce

"Did he write one to me?" I asked.

"No, ma'am." he replied. "Just this one for your daughters." The officer said he needed to talk further with me and would come back in a day or two. I could barely speak. The shock, the fact that Les was actually gone, had paralyzed me.

Now the only thing the girls had left of their father was this hand-written note.

To Sarah & Sophia

Daddy Loves you very much
And I will always love you
No matter where I end up.
Daddy would love to be an angel
And watch out over you two.
I've broken and I can't be fixed
I've tried but it hurts too much
Daddy wants to be free
Don't ever think that I don't love you
And that I didn't want to be there for you
You were the JOY in my life
Sarah and Sophia,
You are the two sweetest girls in the world
You made me laugh so much
And I will surely miss you
Love daddy
Huggs & Kisses

Suicide

Why do you hurt yourself?
I asked the man I love
Why do you want to die
And go away from this life
Unable to watch your children grow?

The emotional pain is too severe
I need to feel physical pain to make it stop
And the guilt that I feel inside
It makes my head want to pop.

He used to love life
And had a zest for all there was
I was his queen, his wife
He loved me, just because.

I don't want to die
But I see no other way to be free
I don't expect you to understand
Just listen to me.

So that's what I did, I listened
And listened some more.
He revealed stories of
Hurt, abuse, drugs, they poured

He explained his pain like pain I'd not known
Begged for my forgiveness
Then said it would be soon
Time to go home.

Kellie JOYce

He talked this way for a couple of years
I hope he'd come to understand
That we are all given what we have
That he was dealt a shitty hand

That life is still a gift
Oh, how I feel that now
'Cause when he jumped off that bridge
He took part of me somehow.

Every day he is with me
For I see him in his kids
All the things they do
Their laughter, sense of humour
Their artistic talents too.

Was it selfish?
Indeed it was not!
His words I listened to
And have not forgotten

The man that taught me
So much of life
Lives within my heart and soul
Lived as only he knew how
Explained it in the stories he told

His life ended
The day he was diagnosed with mental illness
It killed his spirit
His body, his mind
Death was the only happiness he could find.

That was his reality
And he lived life
For as long as he could.

Kellie JOYce – September 1999

Chapter Seventy-Five

I find myself at a crucial junction in my life. It is a beautiful warm fall evening. The leaves are turning and for a short time the world is full of radiant colour. It will soon be the fourteenth anniversary of Les' death. I have very few memories of these past years. I can't recall many pleasant events or situations, as I am still not able to see pictures in my head. The bad events I can pull from a place in my thoughts as if they happened yesterday and I can't seem to get the words on paper fast enough.

It seems I have estranged myself from many of those years the same way I did as a child. My girls have kept me busy, as have my passions that include gardening and photography. My garden is huge and this is where I spend much of my time in the summer, using my camera to capture its beauty. I also photograph just about everything else. I have well over 200 000 photos in my library, and each day I keep taking more pictures to add to my collection. I find that photography is a calming hobby that helps to keep my emotions in balance.

I also like to bake and cook and have excelled in this as well. I sell my goods to people in our local community and send them to my girls' schools to assist in fundraising.

Over the last three years I have spent twenty-four weeks away from home, escaping to faraway places in an effort to try to resolve my mental health issues while awaiting the help I need. Of course I have written, and, as I write this, many other books are floating around in my head.

But suddenly I feel as if I have cracked...

I remember Les' words, "I've broken and I can't be fixed."
Six years ago these words had meaning for me. I could
relate to the way Les had been feeling the night he
jumped two hundred feet from the top of that bridge to
his death. I didn't think of taking my own life, but I will
say that I became someone I no longer recognized. I was
full of anger, rage and pain and no one seemed to
understand. In my home there was very little contact
with the outside world. I didn't allow my children to
watch TV, to listen to the radio, to have a computer or to
read a newspaper. They were allowed to read books, so
that kept them somewhat in touch with the world. As for
myself, I would escape by going to that place in my mind
where I could shut out the world and be alone with my
thoughts. I continued to write in my head. I lived this
way, in an isolated bubble, for a decade and a half.

Kellie JOYce

What Is It?

I get used to the other me
Like bolts of lightning
Surging through my body
No control
Merely numbness
Just half of me
Distressed and alienated
What caused this brutality?
I want to resolve it
And embrace my anatomy
A roadmap to bliss
In another life.

Kellie JOYce - January 1998

Chapter Seventy-Six

The stress I was under caused my body to respond in strange ways and my physical strength was weakening. The neurologists I had seen were all convinced that I was suffering from MS.

But it was Dr. Sureman who gave me the first insight into what was really happening to me. I was once again at the end of my rope and had gone to see yet another neurologist. My symptoms had not progressed like the typical symptoms of MS so my family doctor wanted another opinion. I believe he felt helpless because he did not have the answers to explain all of the negative symptoms that plagued my life. The prime symptom that all the doctors had focused on was the numbness and tingling I felt in my left side. Any exertion would exacerbate this into near paralysis. However, there was a whole list of secondary symptoms. I endured major pain and discomfort in my neck and lower spine. I suffered from lack of sleep, as four hours a night tended to be all I averaged. When I did sleep there were nightmares that would wake me and force me to want to stay awake. I experienced memory loss. It was hard to remember one day's events to the next. I had problems with muscle control that affected my bladder and bowels. Eventually I underwent major surgery to repair a prolapsed bladder. These were just the physical symptoms. The emotional pain I find difficult to put into words. Les' words "I've broken and I can't be fixed" actually sum it up well.

I sat in Dr. Sureman's office, waiting my turn, all the while surveying the room and those in it. I was aware of everything and everyone around me, just as I

Kellie JOYce

remembered having been as a child. This heightened awareness was another of the daily symptoms with which I lived.

I heard rather than saw the receptionist coming down the hall to get me, so I stood up. "You must be Kellie. Follow me," she said. I was taken to a little room that looked like a large square box. I don't recall even seeing a window. There was just a desk and two chairs that faced each other. I felt uncomfortable because there was very little space that separated me from the doctor. He introduced himself and began to read a chart that held report after report of test results from past visits to the other neurologists.

"Have you had much trauma in your life, Kellie?" he asked. I was a little surprised by his question. Why was he asking about my past trauma?

"What do you mean by trauma?" I responded. I wasn't really sure what he was getting at, but his question was evoking an odd response in my body.

"I mean were you ever sexually abused or abandoned, lose a loved one, parents divorce, those kinds of things?"

"Well, yeah, but hasn't everyone? And what does this have to do with my MS?" I asked him.

He continued to read more of the reports. Then he laid all the papers down on the desk, looked straight at me and said, "I don't feel that you have MS at all. I believe your body is responding to trauma."

196

"Are you saying that what I am experiencing is not real and that I don't have all these symptoms and the pain?" I asked in disbelief.

"Oh, no," he answered. "The tests do show your symptoms are very real and I believe everything you are telling me, but I don't believe you are suffering from MS. You see, the symptoms of MS get worse over time. Yours have remained consistent over the past six or seven years. You need to deal with the traumas that plague you, and then the symptoms and the pain will go away."

At this point my anger had escalated to the breaking point and I didn't listen to anything else he had to say. I told him I thought he was full of shit (in a round-about way) and stormed out of his office.

I refused to go to any more doctors. But I started thinking. What if Dr. Sureman was right? That thought lingered in my mind. Could I heal myself like he had suggested? It was worth a try. So for the next six months I forced myself to walk to and from the post office every day. On a good day it would normally take about ten minutes to walk there and back, but, with my spine the way it was and with my level of pain, it could easily take forty-five minutes to an hour.

In time my friends started to notice a difference in my mobility, and I too, was starting to think that maybe there was some truth in what the doctor had said. I had conversation after conversation with myself. "Maybe he wasn't as condescending as I had first thought. Is it possible that I have been misdiagnosed all these years and that I don't have MS? Now that would be something good to come out of this."

It was enough to make me want to fight back! I told myself that if there was a way for me to get better, to heal myself, I was going to try. And so my journey began.

Chapter Seventy-Seven

I didn't tell anyone what I was doing. It took me about two years to fully regain my strength and the use of all my muscles. With that came a greater desire to want to understand the emotional damage that occurs when one is faced with one trauma after another. I thought the best way to try and understand was by returning to Newfoundland with my girls to see if I could put some final closure to my emotional turmoil.

My trip home was one of deep awakening and it was actually a trigger that intensified my symptoms. My anger surfaced and my fear brought me back to the age of eleven, the same age as my oldest daughter is now. It was the age when my father had brutally raped and threatened to kill me. I did not fully understand what was happening to me. I felt like I was going mad. The emotional pain caused me to suffer severe depression and I didn't want to be around anyone, not even my children.

I returned home and locked myself in my room for months on end. I spent day and night in an isolated state. Finally I realized that I needed help and that I couldn't continue living this way. I went to my family doctor and told him what was happening. He referred me to a psychologist in Guelph, a city close to where I lived. I needed to understand what was happening to me, so I took the next available appointment and went to see the psychologist.

Her name was Laura and she worked at Stonewood Health Centre, the same place Les had been. She was a short, plump lady with a huge smile. She spoke in a soft and calming tone. I immediately felt comfortable with her. I even forgot that I was at Stonewood.

"Kellie, this first session will last about four hours. You will be given booklets containing several hundred questions and I ask that you answer them and then we can discuss them. Are you up for that?"

"Anything," I told her. "I will do anything to understand what is happening to me."

That was the first visit. There were a few more sessions after that and then it was time for my evaluation. I remember that Laura asked me if I knew what the letters PTSD meant. I quickly responded, "People Talking Sharing Dreaming."

She laughed, thinking this was a clever response. She told me that the acronym stood for Post Traumatic Stress Disorder. "This is what you are suffering from, Kellie. PTSD."

I cried like a big baby in her office that day when she described PTSD. She continued by saying that there was an eight-week program at Stonewood from which I would benefit. She said she would send a referral to my doctor, then handed me a brochure that read:

Life after Trauma

PTSD is characterized by
- Intrusive symptoms such as memories, night-mares or physical sensations.

- Avoidance of people, places or situations that remind the individual of the traumatic incident.
- Diminished responsiveness to the outside world, such as detachment, loss of interest in previously enjoyed activities, inability to experience emotions or intimacy.
- Symptoms of increased arousal, difficulty sleeping or concentrating and intense mood fluctuations.

"Read it out loud," Laura instructed. "I want to hear you say it." As I read the brochure outlining the symptoms of PTSD, my crying intensified. I realized that everything I was reading related to me. I wasn't going crazy, and my symptoms were actually caused by something that had a name. It was liberating to be able to put a name to the madness that goes on in my head every minute of every day and to know that my pain had a cause. I had PTSD, but now what? What comes next?

The 'what comes next' was the wait. The real pain would come with the perpetual wait and the implications that this new label would have on my life. I did not have the proper medical insurance or the financial means to take part in the treatment I needed. This is where I find myself today.

I sit here, not with a broken leg waiting to be rushed to the hospital where a cast would allow healing in six to eight weeks, or with diabetes where I would be given a pump or insulin to regulate my sugar count. No, I sit here with mental illness caused by Post Traumatic Stress Disorder. And because one cannot physically see any damage, I feel my rights to get the medical attention I need and deserve are being ignored.

Chapter Seventy-Eight

I am still on the wait list for the PTSD program at Stonewood Health Centre. It has been over five years. I am not alone in my frustration regarding the wait time for medical attention for those of us dealing with mental illness. In fact, fifteen years ago the same problem existed. The ignorance, lack of funding, shame and stigma relating to mental illness were huge factors in the loss of my children's father. Today my girls sit back helplessly as they watch their mother struggle with similar issues regarding the way people with mental illness are viewed and how they are treated by our health care system.

My oldest daughter, Sarah, opens the door to my room, sticks her head in and asks, "May I talk to you, Mom?"

"Sure, honey. Come on in."

She sits down at my bedside and asks, "How's your book coming, Mom?"

"I'm almost done, sweetie. Why?" I ask.

"I want to read it, Mom. I know what I told you a few months ago, but I've changed my mind. I want to read it all. I want everyone to know my dad. You can use our real names, Mom, if you want."

"That won't be necessary," I tell her. "I will let you be the first to read the book, honey, as soon as it is edited."

She opens her arms and hugs me as she says, "Thanks, Mom. I'm so proud of you!"

This is a grown-up moment for my seventeen year-old daughter and me. I want to get well so we can have more of these beautiful moments.

Chapter Seventy-Nine

Today, as I continue 'the wait' to enter the trauma program, I have joined a hospice group to discuss regulating emotions. The group consists of fourteen women and we are all there for the same reason. We are trying to understand the damage that complex trauma can do to the brain and how it can be reversed. Each week we learn a new tool that we have to practise in order to help our brains get back to a healthy state. I wish students could learn this in school, as it is an education from which we all could benefit.

I know it is never too late to heal. I am happy to report that this group is helping me immensely. I am learning to be mindful and live in the moment. The more I practise, the healthier I become.

Face it! It is a sad fact. An estimated 75% of people living with mental illness around the world will never receive any treatment. Increasing the access to mental health services AND removing the stigma associated with mental illness is essential if we expect to one day change this frustrating statistic!

I want that day to be NOW!

Who Am I?

I am a tree with many branches
And I have survived quite a few storms
I have strong recollection
Of the showers and showers
That have poured over me
And have taken some time to dry off
Those who sat under me
During the stormy weather
Felt little shade, little shelter and
No compassion
Today I enJOY the pleasures
I give and receive from those around me
The fear of the storms are slowly fading
And I am starting to trust
In others and myself
Who am I?
I am a tree continuing to grow

Kellie JOYce

Epilogue

In 2012 the Mental Health Commission of Canada's (MHCC) Knowledge Exchange Centre (KEC) launched its inaugural SPARK Training Institute. The nine-month mentorship had an overall goal of improving the capacity for implementing effective knowledge exchange practices in the field of mental health, substance abuse and addictions. I was one of forty individuals chosen from across Canada to participate in this select group. We were asked to do a project within our means to help promote change and, in some way, help stop the shame and stigma surrounding mental health. My project has been the writing of this book and the sharing of my story.

Les, my late husband and the father of my children, was born December 15, 1960. This year he would have been fifty-four years old. My way of honouring his life and the impact that he has had on mine is the publishing of my memoir. I can still hear my father's voice, "You're a nobody. You're stupid. You'll never amount to anything." But I won't let this stop me from fighting for my emotional freedom. I am somebody. I am intelligent. And I have the freedom to be whatever it is I want to be and to go wherever it is I want to go. However, without my health, I truly am not alive, merely existing in a prison of emotional pain. I want to be free, but not in death as Les chose to be free. I want to be free in life.

It is not enough for me to just tell my story. I want all of you, my readers, to hear my heart. It aches for fairness, for justice and for change. By sharing my story I hope to inspire you and show the importance of coming out of this closet. We who suffer from mental illness have rights too. We have the right to proper medical care. We have the right to have equal opportunity in the job force. And we have the right to live a life where shame and stigma are no more.

This book was not written for anybody; it was written for everybody: parents, teachers, government officials, judges, those in the mental health sector and yes, all of you! I share with you in the hope that it will spark change and promote healing for everyone who suffers from this cruel affliction.

Society could look the other way and allow the ones who suffer to remain alone amid their stories of anguish and pain. We have been doing that for centuries. Or we could start talking, sharing and taking action. How much effort would it really take for us to open our eyes and our hearts and respond to the children who are living in a dysfunctional environment like the one in which I lived? How many of us dealing with mental illness will not seek treatment because of the way we are frowned upon by society as a whole?

There are those who would call what I have 'complex trauma'. Others put a name to it and call it mental illness, PTSD, or worse yet, as I have been called, a freak or a disturbed individual. The reality is that we are all products of our environment, and we must deal with and cope with the real life situations that face us in the present. This is called survival.

I truly believe that it is through sharing our personal stories that real change takes place.

Kellie JOYce

I cannot bring Les back, but what I can do is honour his memory and hope that others will learn from the story of his tragic death. The gift of life that was stolen from him must not be stolen from anyone else. Faith can be restored to those dealing with mental illness if we all start speaking out and showing our face. My name is Kellie JOYce. I am a writer and a photographer and I have PTSD: People - Talking - Sharing - Dreaming. Now that is a label I do not mind owning. For me, and I hope for others, it is the path to freedom, health and justice.

Kellie JOYce
September 2014